THE COMPLETE
SLOW COOKER

THE COMPLETE
SLOW COOKER

Packed with recipes, techniques, and tips

Sara Lewis

hamlyn

An Hachette UK Company
www.hachette.co.uk

First published in Great Britain in 2010 by
Hamlyn, a division of Octopus Publishing Group Ltd
Endeavour House
189 Shaftesbury Avenue
London
WC2H 8JG
www.octopusbooksusa.com

Distributed in the U.S. and Canada by Octopus Books USA:
c/o Hachette Book Group
237 Park Avenue
New York, NY 10017

Sara Lewis asserts the moral right to be identified
as the author of this work

ISBN 978-0-600-62166-9

A CIP catalog record for this book is available
from the Library of Congress

Printed and bound in China

10 9 8 7 6 5 4 3 2

Standard level spoon measures are used in all recipes.

Medium eggs have been used throughout.
Fresh herbs should be used unless otherwise stated.

A few recipes contain nuts and nut derivatives. Anyone with a
known nut allergy must avoid these.

This book contains some dishes made with raw or lightly cooked
eggs. It is prudent for more vulnerable people such as pregnant and
nursing mothers, invalids, the elderly, babies, and young children to
avoid raw or lightly cooked eggs.

Read your slow cooker manual before you begin and preheat
the slow cooker if required according to the manufacturer's
instructions. Because slow cookers vary slightly from
manufacturer to manufacturer, check recipe timings with the
manufacturer's directions for a recipe using the same ingredients.

All recipes for this book were tested in oval-shaped slow cookers
with a working capacity of 2½ quarts and total capacity of 3½ quarts.
Where the slow cooker recipe is finished off under the broiler, hold
the pot with dishtowels to remove it from the machine housing.

Contents

Introduction

If you've just bought your first slow cooker, congratulations. You're going to enjoy plenty of delicious and succulent meals. Before you use your cooker for the first time, however, read this introduction so that you get the best from it.

Slow cooking

If you were brought up by a parent who was a believer in slow cooking—and who probably still has their first slow cooker, which could now be over 30 years old and still going strong—then you'll appreciate what it was like to come home to a properly cooked supper.

Now you can do the same for yourself and your family no matter how pushed for time you are or how late you are working in the evening. Slow-cooked dishes are back in vogue once again, and cuts of meat, such as slow-cooked pork, which several years ago would have been laughed at, are now appearing on the menus of many a smart restaurant. From pot-roasts and preserves to braised oxtail and one-pot dinners, timeless classic family meals are more popular than ever. More importantly, these are the kind of dishes that can easily and simply be prepared at home, and a slow cooker has become an essential kitchen utensil for the 21st century.

The appeal of slow cookers

What is the slow cooker phenomenon all about? The main appeal is that it cooks food so slowly that the food doesn't boil dry and can be left unattended for 8–10 hours without any danger that it will boil over or burn on the bottom of the pan. That said, some ingredients do need to be fried first, but then you simply add everything to the slow cooker and get on with the rest of the day.

If the convenience isn't enough to persuade you, then you will find that the flavor you can achieve is second to none. Meaty casseroles or dishes infused with spices and herbs seem to melt in the mouth. You can also save money by using less well known, cheaper cuts of meat, such as neck of lamb, rabbit, and bacon hocks, and even Sunday lunch—half a shoulder of lamb, a braised brisket of beef, or a pot-roast chicken—can be easily prepared in a slow cooker.

Not only is a slow cooker easy to use, but it will enhance the flavor of your food and is cheap to run (costing about the same price as a lightbulb), thereby saving fuel, which is good for the environment.

Saving time

Although the idea of getting supper ready before you go out in the morning may seem like the last thing you want to do or can fit in, once you have tried it a few times, you will be won round. Spending just 15–20 minutes early in the day will enable you to prepare supper in your slow cooker, leaving you time to get on with something else. If you have a young family, supper can be put on after the morning school run so that it is ready when you and the children are at your most exhausted in the late afternoon. If you are working shifts or if you are a student with a busy day of lectures, you could put on a meal before you go out so that a hot supper is waiting when you get back home. If you are new to retirement, supper can be left to cook while you enjoy a relaxing day playing golf or tackling a DIY project.

How to use this book

This book will guide you through the range of dishes you can make with a slow cooker, helping you understand how to get the most out of this versatile cooking tool. There are recipes for everyday favorites as well as for dishes to share with friends, such as Salmon-wrapped Cod with Buttered Leeks (see pages 176–177) or Venison Puff Pie (see pages 170–171). There are also plenty of vegetarian treats, such as Eggplant Ratatouille with Ricotta Dumplings (see pages 142–143) and Balsamic Tomatoes with Spaghetti (see pages 148–149).

As well as basic safety and start-up advice, there is also advice on different ways to use a slow cooker and how it can change your cooking lifestyle. To make puddings such as Christmas Pudding (see pages 212–213) you can simply put a pudding mold directly onto the base of the slow cooker pot and add water. You can also use a slow cooker as a bain marie or water bath to cook baked custards, pâtés, and terrines. Pour mixtures of alcohol and fruit juice into the pot and heat them up to make warming hot party punches or hot toddies, which can be ladled out as required. You will find that you can easily make a wide variety of dishes such as chocolate or cheese fondues, preserves and simple chutneys, or even boil up the bones or a chicken carcass to make homemade stock.

There is also a chapter of recipes for short-cut suppers (see pages 98–119), which don't involve browning the meat beforehand, and, if you are really short of time, there is a chapter of cheat's recipes (see pages 232–251) that make good use of ready-made jars, cans, and chilled extras.

A new lifestyle

Although your friends might tease you about how long your casseroles have been in the oven, once you have experienced the advantages of using a slow cooker you will find that it suits your way of life. You might even find that you will take your slow cooker on self-catering vacations: after a busy day on the beach or sight-seeing, there are few things more welcoming than the aroma of supper bubbling away. Slow cookers don't just mean winter stews, as the recipe for Smoked Cod with Cannellini Bean Mash (see pages 104–105) proves.

Whatever your circumstances, slow cooking can be a lifesaver. They are environmentally friendly, cheap to run, won't boil dry, and are incredibly versatile—everyone should have one. So, put the meal on, take the dog out for a walk, put the children to bed or have a glass of wine in the garden ... and supper is ready when you are.

Slow cooker basics

Choosing a slow cooker

The best and most versatile slow cookers are oval in shape. They are ideal for cooking a whole chicken, have ample room for a large pudding mold or four individual molds and are capacious enough to make soup for six people.

Slow cookers are available in three sizes and are measured in total capacity; the size is usually printed on the packaging with the working capacity or the maximum space for food:

* for two people choose a mini oval slow cooker with a maximum capacity of $1\frac{1}{2}$ quarts and a working capacity of 1 quart

* for four people choose either a round or a more versatile oval cooker with a total capacity of $3\frac{1}{2}$ quarts and a working capacity of $2\frac{1}{2}$ quarts

* for six people choose a large, oval slow cooker with a total capacity of 5 quarts and a working capacity of 4 quarts or the extra large, round $6\frac{1}{2}$ quart cooker with a working capacity of $4\frac{1}{2}$ quarts.

Perhaps surprisingly, the very large slow cookers cost only a little more than the medium-size models, and so it is easy to be swept along thinking that they are better value for money. Unless you have a large family or like to cook large quantities so that you have enough

supper for one meal with extra portions to freeze, you will probably find that they are too big for your everyday needs. Remember that you need to half-fill a slow cooker when cooking meat, fish, or vegetable dishes.

Before you begin

Although it might seem obvious, always check that the meat, pudding mold, soufflé dish, or individual molds will fit into your slow cooker pot before you begin, to avoid frustration when you are halfway through making a recipe.

PREHEATING

It is important that you read the manual or handbook that came with your slow cooker before you begin cooking. Some manufacturers recommend preheating the slow cooker on the high setting for a minimum of 20 minutes before food is added. The majority however, recommend that the slow cooker is heated only when it has been filled with food.

Changing recipes for a different cooker size

All the recipes in this book have been tested in a standard-size slow cooker with a total capacity of $3\frac{1}{2}$ quarts. If you have a 5 quart six-portion cooker or a $1\frac{1}{2}$ quart two-person cooker you can adapt the recipes in this book by simply halving the ingredients for two portions or adding half as much again to the recipe for six, keeping the timings the same. All the recipes made in a pudding mold, soufflé dish, or individual molds may also be cooked in a larger slow cooker for the same length of time.

SAFETY FIRST

Before you start to use the slow cooker put it on the work surface, somewhere out of the way, and make sure that the flex is tucked around the back of the machine and not trailing over the front of the work surface or near the stovetop.

The outside of the slow cooker does get hot, so wear oven mitts when you lift the pot out of the housing to serve. Set it onto a heatproof mat on the table or work surface to serve the food. If the slow cooker lid has a vent in the top, make sure that the cooker is not placed under an eye-level cabinet or the steam might catch someone's arm as they reach into the cabinet.

Never reheat cooked food in a slow cooker. Heat up a cooked casserole in a saucepan on the stove and make sure to bring it to a boil and cook it through thoroughly. Only reheat cooked food once.

Slow cooker techniques

Basic frying preparation

There are two basic approaches. You can fry the meat, then add onions and flavorings. Stir in flour at this point, then add stock and flavorings. Bring the mixture to a boil, then spoon it into the slow cooker pot.

This method arguably gives the best flavor and color, but the idea of frying meat and onions first thing in the morning can be a bit off-putting, and if you prefer you can prepare all the ingredients the night before. Mix ingredients such as flavorings in a bowl, cover with plastic wrap, and chill in the refrigerator. Don't be tempted to part-fry meat and chill it. In the morning add the ingredients to the slow cooker pot without frying anything first, and then add hot liquid, heated in the microwave, in a saucepan, or by crumbling a bouillon cube into a cup and mixing with boiling water. Depending on the recipe, you might want to increase the cooking time by 1–2 hours.

Liquid is key

A slow cooker is really like a large insulated saucepan, and although it must never be used without added liquid, the amount needed is less than when you are simmering a pan on the stove for several hours because there is no danger that it will boil dry. As the casserole

heats up, the liquid turns to steam, which condenses on the lid and falls back into the pot, which is the reason why you need less stock. Because the heat is constant you can safely leave the machine on even when you are not in the house.

Filling the pot

When you buy a slow cooker you will find, confusingly, that the manufacturer has put two figures on the side of the box. The lower figure is the space for cooking, and the higher figure is the total capacity of the slow cooker pot.

Aim to fill the slow cooker pot between half and three-quarters full. Joints of meat should fill no more than two-thirds of the pot. If you are using a pudding mold or ovenproof dish allow ½ inch at the narrowest point in an oval pot or ¾ inch in a round one. If you are making soup the pot can be a little fuller, but make sure that the liquid level is no higher than 1 inch from the top.

Heat settings

All slow cookers have a "high," "low," and "off" setting, and some models also have either "medium," "warm," or "auto" settings. In general, the high setting will take only half the time of the low setting when you are cooking a casserole containing diced meat or vegetables. This can be useful if you plan to eat at lunchtime or get delayed in starting the casserole. Both settings will reach just below 212°F or boiling point during cooking, but when set to "high" the temperature is reached more quickly.

An auto setting, although not crucial, is helpful if you plan to add meat without frying it first because it starts the slow cooker on high then automatically reduces the heat to low by means of a thermostat. The auto setting is also useful if the slow cooker is very full. If you don't have this facility start the recipe on high for 30 minutes, then reduce the heat manually before you leave the house.

Increasing the temperature from low to high at the end of a recipe can be useful if you want to thicken the casserole with cornstarch at the end of cooking, add extra green vegetables, or reheat soups that have been pureed and then returned to the slow cooker pot.

The warm setting is suitable once the maximum cooking time is reached, to keep the food on hold, which is convenient for late diners but not essential, because the low setting will not cause foods to spoil unless they are rice based.

Cooking times

The slow cooker will help you to make the most of your time. The table below shows how long different types of food, and some recipes in this book, take in the slow cooker, and at what setting, so that you can plan your time in and out of the kitchen. These timings show how long the food takes to cook in the slow cooker. Initial preparation and final touches such as browning under the broiler and preparing accompaniments are not included.

Cook on low

1–2 hours
Poached halved bananas, apple wedges or halved peaches, Chocolate Puddings (pages 192–193)

2–3 hours
Fish soups, fruit compotes, rice pudding made with risotto rice rather than pudding rice, Crème Caramels (pages 194–195), Honeyed Rice Pudding (page 198)

3–4 hours
Squid, poached pear halves, individual crème brûlées, lemon curd, Mackerel Kedgeree (pages 94–95)

4–5 hours
Cheesy macaroni, vegetable soups without potatoes, stuffed peppers, bread and butter pudding, Tuna Arrabiata (pages 84–85)

6–8 hours
Sausages, diced boneless chicken and boneless chicken breasts, soups with diced potato, vegetable stews, curries, and gnocchi, meatballs, Barley Risotto with Blue Cheese Butter (pages 100–101)

8–10 hours
Casseroles or soups with diced meat, ground beef and lamb, sliced lamb loin, whole lamb leg steaks or chump chops, pork shoulder steaks or boneless pork chops, chicken thighs and drumsticks on the bone, oxtail, bean stews, marmalade base

Cook on high

Under 1 hour
Cheese or chocolate fondue, Eggs en Cocotte with Smoked Salmon (pages 40–41)

1–2 hours
Oatmeal, soused herrings, whole trout, 1 lb thick piece salmon fillet, Zucchini & Fava Bean Frittata (pages 48–49), Eggplant Timbale (pages 158–159)

2–3 hours
Corn chili, kidneys, braised red cabbage or diced beets, cheesecake, fruit jellies and conserves, individual puddings, Mediterranean Roasted Vegetable Terrine (pages 52–53)

3–4 hours
Whole boneless chicken breasts, 1 lb haggis, 1½ lb whole pheasant, lentil dhal, tomato pasta sauce, 5–7 cup steamed pudding, Eggplant Ratatouille with Ricotta Dumplings (pages 142–143)

4–5 hours
Spanish baked potatoes, braised celery, Lemon & Poppy Seed Drizzle Cake (pages 210–211)

5–6 hours
Pork ribs, lamb shanks, duck legs, rillettes, meatloaf and pâté, ox tongue, 5 cup steak and kidney pudding, 2 lb whole guinea fowl, 3 lb whole chicken, Duck, Pork, & Apple Rillettes (pages 54–55)

6–7 hours
2½ lb ham joint, 2 lb pork or ham hock, neck of lamb on the bone, breast of lamb, turkey drumstick, 2 lb beef brisket, chutney

7–8 hours
Hotpot with sliced potato topping, 1¾ lb piece thick pork belly, half a shoulder of lamb, 6 cup Christmas pudding, Minted Lamb with Beet Couscous (pages 178–179)

What to cook at what setting

All the recipes in this book show a span of cooking time, which means the dish will be cooked and ready to eat at the shorter time but can be left without spoiling for an extra hour or so.

Pieces of meat can be cooked on low or high, but larger joints must be cooked on high so that they are cooked right through. If you are not sure how long to cook something, err on the generous side because the heat is so gentle that even food that has been in longer than really necessary will not dry out.

If you are unsure if meat is cooked through cut into the thickest part of the chicken, rabbit, pheasant, guinea fowl, or pork: the juices should run clear with no hint of pink. Beef and lamb can be eaten slightly pink so it isn't so crucial for them. Make doubly sure with a meat thermometer if you don't feel confident. Fish should break easily into pieces and the flakes should be the same color all the way through.

Adjusting the cooking time

If you want to slow down or speed up timings for diced meat or vegetable casseroles so that they fit around your plans better, adjust the heat settings and timings as suggested below:

Cook on low	Cook on medium	Cook on high
6–8 hours	4–6 hours	3–4 hours
8–10 hours	6–8 hours	5–6 hours
10–12 hours	8–10 hours	7–8 hours

Note: These timings were taken from the Morphy Richards slow cooker instruction handbook. Do not change timings or settings for fish, whole joints, or dairy dishes in recipes.

Slow cooker ingredients

Meat

To make sure that meat is properly cooked cut it into equal-size pieces so that cooking is even and fry meat before adding to the slow cooker.

A whole guinea fowl or pheasant, even a small ham joint or half a shoulder of lamb can also be cooked in an oval slow cooker pot, but make sure that it does not fill more than the lower two-thirds of the pot, then cover with boiling liquid and cook on high. Check that the

meat is cooked before serving either by using a meat thermometer or inserting a skewer through the thickest part and checking that the juices run clear.

Add boiling stock or sauce to the slow cooker pot and press the meat beneath the surface of the hot stock before cooking begins.

Vegetables and fruit

Surprisingly, root vegetables can take longer to cook than meat, so make sure that you cut them into small enough pieces. The amount of liquid and size of the vegetable chunks greatly affects the speed of cooking in a slow cooker: the more liquid and the smaller the size of vegetable chunk, the quicker the cooking. Denser root vegetables take almost the same time to cook as diced beef.

If you are adding vegetables to a meaty casserole, make sure that the pieces are a little smaller than the meat, and try to keep all the vegetable chunks the same size so that they cook evenly. Press the vegetables and meat below the surface of the liquid with the back of a spoon before cooking commences.

If you are making soup, puree it while it is still in the slow cooker pot using an electric stick blender if you have one. Or transfer the soup to a freestanding blender or food processor, blend, and return to the slow cooker.

Cut potatoes will turn black if they not cooked beneath stock, so make sure that you press them beneath the surface of the stock before cooking. Apples, pears, and bananas will also discolor, so toss them in a little lemon juice before cooking.

Slow cooker basics

* Foods cooked in a slow cooker must contain some liquid.
* Foods will not brown during cooking, so fry foods before they go in or brown the top by transferring the slow cooker pot from its housing to the broiler just before serving. Alternatively, use a kitchen torch.
* The smaller the pieces of food the quicker they will cook.
* Food at the bottom of the slow cooker pot will cook more quickly, so put root vegetables into the pot first.

Fish

The slow, gentle cooking means that individual pieces of fish or a larger 1 lb piece will not break up or overcook. Make sure that the fish is covered by the hot liquid so that it cooks evenly.

Add peeled shrimp or shelled mussels to a tomato-based pasta sauce or soup at the end of cooking and cook on high for 20–30 minutes until piping hot.

If you are using frozen fish it must be thoroughly defrosted, rinsed with cold water and drained before cooking. Bags of frozen mixed shellfish which contain sliced squid, shelled mussels, and shrimp must also be defrosted thoroughly before use.

Lentils and legumes

Canned beans have been used in the recipes in this book because they are quick and convenient, but if you prefer to use dried beans soak them overnight in cold water. Drain them, then tip them into a saucepan and cover with fresh water. Bring to a boil and boil rapidly for 10 minutes. Drain again and add to the slow cooker pot with the other ingredients and cover with hot stock. Cook on high for 6–7 hours.

Pearl barley and red, Puy, or green lentils do not need soaking overnight, but if you are not sure check the instructions on the package. These can be cooked on low.

Rice

Easy-cook rice is preferable for slow cookers because it has been partially cooked during manufacture. Some of the starch has been washed off, making it less sticky when cooked.

Thickening casseroles

Casseroles can be thickened in the same way as if you were cooking conventionally. You can do this before slow cooking, by adding the flour after searing the meat or frying the onions, then gradually mixing in the stock. You can mix cornflour with a little water and stir in the mixture 15–30 minutes (on high) or 30–60 minutes (on low) before the end of cooking. Alternatively, pour off the liquid from the cooked dish into a saucepan or frying pan and boil on the hob to reduce. Because the liquid does not evaporate during cooking as it would on the hob, there is no need to lift the lid and check on the stew's progress or top up with stock during cooking. You will probably find that you can use less stock than you would normally do, but it is important that the meat and vegetables are covered with stock so that they cook evenly.

When you are cooking rice allow a minimum of 1 cup water for each $1/2$ cup of easy-cook rice or up to 2 cups water for the same quantity of risotto rice. You can make risottos in a slow cooker, but unlike making them in a skillet, when the warm stock is added ladle by ladle, you will need to add all the stock in one go.

Use risotto rice when you make rice puddings because it cooks more quickly than the more traditional round-grain pudding rice.

Pasta

For best results cook the pasta separately in a saucepan of boiling water and then mix with the casserole just before serving. Small pasta shapes, such as macaroni or shells, can be added to soups 20–30 minutes before the end of cooking, as in Chicken & Noodle Broth (see page 35).

Cream and milk

Use whole milk or heavy cream, which are less likely to separate. Cream and milk are usually added at the beginning of cooking only in rice pudding or baked egg custard-style dishes.

If you are making soup add the milk at the end, when the soup has been pureed. Stir cream into soups just 15 minutes before the end of cooking or swirl over the soup when you have ladled it into soup bowls.

Using ready-made sauces

Simply fry the meat and onions as you would if you were going to cook them in the oven. Add the sauce and bring to a boil, then transfer to the slow cooker pot.

If you prefer not to fry the meat first, put it straight into the slow cooker pot with any vegetables and bring the sauce to a boil in a bowl in the microwave or a saucepan on the stovetop. Pour the sauce over the meat in the slow cooker and then cook at the setting and for the time recommended in the table on page 13. If the sauce seems a little thick don't be tempted to add more liquid because the juices from the meat will thin it during cooking.

You will need a 13 oz jar or can or larger for 4 chops, 4 chicken breasts, or 1 lb of ground meat. The sauce must be hot when you add it to the slow cooker. Don't be tempted to add salt to recipes made with bought sauces or soups because these will be seasoned already.

Adapting your own recipes

If you have a favorite recipe, perhaps from a TV chef, one given to you by a friend or handed down within your family, and you feel it would cook perfectly in the slow cooker, then try adapting it.

Look at the table on page 13 and compare the ingredients in your recipe with the same main ingredient. Check with the ingredients list in the manufacturer's handbook, which will indicate the quantity that will fit in the slow cooker pot and the appropriate timing for the main ingredient.

You will probably need to reduce the amount of liquid that the recipes use. However, some slow cooker lids don't seem to fit as well as others, and these models may need topping up with a little extra stock if you are cooking on high. Placing a folded dishtowel on top of the lid will help to make a better seal. As with any kind of cooker, you need to get to know your own model.

Adjusting liquid levels

You can add extra flavor to basic recipes with a little wine, some beer, or some dry cider. If you are adding lots of fresh tomatoes remember that these will make extra juice as they turn to pulp during cooking.

If you haven't got the liquid levels quite right, add a little hot stock at the end of cooking or when you notice that things look a bit dry. If there is too much sauce at the end, pour it into a saucepan and boil rapidly for 5–10 minutes to reduce it. Or, if you prefer, thicken it with a little cornstarch mixed to a paste with some water, stirring this into the slow cooker and cooking on high for 15–30 minutes. Stir again just before serving.

Getting the ingredients right

Remember that any kind of meat or vegetable casserole, stew, or curry can be adapted successfully. Find a recipe with a similar main ingredient in the book or your slow cooker handbook so that you can gauge the amount that will fit into the slow cooker pot and help you work out the cooking time.

Cut down the amount of liquid by one-third, possibly even by half if you are using fresh tomatoes, but bear in mind that you must never use the slow cooker without any liquid.

Meat doesn't have to be fried first, but hot stock or sauce must always be added when you are cooking savory dishes. Remember to cut meat and vegetables into even-size chunks and make sure that root vegetables are in smaller pieces and that you put them in the bottom of the slow cooker where it is hotter so that they cook faster.

If you use your slow cooker as a water bath for steamed puddings, pâtés, meatloaf, or a cake, check that the dish will fit into the slow cooker pot before you begin. There is nothing more frustrating than finding that it won't fit when you have made the recipe and are ready to cook it.

Making the most of your slow cooker

Slow cookers are not just for cooking casseroles and stews for your main meal but are great for preparing a meal at anytime of the day.

Breakfast

Treat yourself to a cooked breakfast if you have a particularly early start or long drive ahead of you. Put breakfast on before you go to bed. Sausage or frankfurter and bean mixtures make good breakfasts, as do dried fruit compotes, which are delicious topped with spoonfuls of yogurt and honey.

You can cook oatmeal overnight, but mix milk with water because the long cooking causes the milk to denature. Alternatively, use longlife milk, which has been heat treated, and sweeten the oatmeal just before serving. If you prefer, try Banana & Cinnamon Oatmeal (see pages 42–43), which can be made in the morning with boiling water. Put it on when you first get up, go for a jog or walk the dog and come back to a healthy breakfast.

Soups

Give your family hearty soups by making homemade chicken stock with the remains of a chicken carcass from the Sunday roast. Strain the liquid, then add rice, pasta, lentils, barley, or mixed vegetables. There are no end of appetizing variations. You can puree the soup or leave it chunky if you prefer.

If you are really hungry add mini meatballs or dumplings or drop in a raw egg and leave it until it is cooked through. Top soup with toasted croutons spread with olive tapenade, pesto, or a sprinkling of cheese, baked puff pastry shapes, or croutons rubbed with a cut garlic clove and fried in olive oil.

Pâtés, potted meat, and meatloaf

You can easily make pâtes, potted meat, and meatloaf by using the slow cooker as a bain marie or water bath. Check that the dish will fit in your slow cooker before you begin—a round, soufflé-style dish is ideal—line it with bacon and fill with a coarse or fine pâté and bake until firm and the juices run clear. Try Turkey & Cranberry Meatloaf (see pages 56–57) or make Eggplant Timbale (see page 158–159).

Egg custards

Bake delicious individual egg custards and brûlées in a water bath. The gentle heat of the slow cooker gives them a perfect finish. Cover with foil so that the condensation doesn't drip into the custard and bake until just set. For an individual custard allow 2½–3½ hours on low.

> ### Lifting pudding molds
> Lift a large mold into the slow cooker by tying string around the edge of the mold and making a string handle. Although this is not crucial when you are adding a cold mold to the slow cooker, it's invaluable when the mold is hot at the end of cooking. Alternatively, use two strips of folded foil, set at right angles to each other, and twist the ends together to make a harness.

Puddings

In winter what could be better than a wonderful sweet or savory pudding? Line a large pudding mold with suet crust pastry and either fill with sliced sirloin steak and a rich gravy or cook mushrooms and chestnuts in a rich red wine sauce.

For satisfying desserts soak raisins in rum to make a grown-up version of "spotted dick" or try Sticky Marmalade Syrup Pudding (see pages 200–201).

Preserves

You can create perfect small gifts for friends in your slow cooker by making homemade jams and preserves. Although a slow cooker will not be able to boil a jam rapidly to setting point, it's perfect for the first stage when slowly simmering whole oranges for marmalade or cooking windfall apples, quinces, or other orchard fruits for jellies.

You can also make chutneys and softly set fruit conserves, such as Apricot Conserve (see page 224), for which a mix of fresh and dried fruits are cooked together. Although it's not a true jam, the dried fruits swell to give a thick, spreadable jam that stores well in the refrigerator. You can also easily make lemon curd, for which the slow cooker is used rather like a double boiler or water bath, eliminating the danger of overheating and curdling the eggs.

Drinks

While away a cold damp Sunday afternoon with the newspapers, an old film on TV, and a glass or two of Hot Buttered Rum (see page 230). If you are hosting a winter party serve a hot drink such as Mulled Wine (see page 227), which can be made in advance and then left to slowly simmer. As guests arrive, remove the lid and allow them to help themselves or refill glasses when needed.

Making the most of casseroles

There are plenty of ways you can make a basic casserole more special or more filling by adding extra toppings toward the end of the cooking time.

MASHED POTATOES

Add a topping of mashed potatoes and a sprinkling of cheese, take the slow cooker pot out of the housing and brown the cheese under the broiler. Because the pot is so deep it may not fit under a conventional separate broiler, but it will fit into an oven with an integral broiler.

DUMPLINGS

Make dumplings with half the quantity of suet to self-rising flour and mix with 1 tablespoon cold water for every ¼ cup of flour. You can leave dumplings plain or flavor them with chopped herbs, mustard or crushed pepper, and lemon zest. Shape them into balls about the size of a walnut, add to the hot casserole and cook on low for about 1 hour or on high for 30–40 minutes until well risen and dry to the touch.

SCONES

Flavor a basic scone recipe with grated cheddar, Parmesan, or crumbled blue cheese or with chopped walnuts, basil, sun-dried tomatoes, or black pitted olives. Cut the scone dough into circles or wedges, arrange them on your casserole and cook on high for 45–60 minutes until well risen. Brush with egg before browning under the broiler.

PUFF PASTRY

Roll out some prepared puff pastry on a lightly floured surface and cut it into an oval about the size of your slow cooker. Transfer it to a greased baking sheet, brush with beaten egg, then leave it as it is or sprinkle with some torn thyme leaves and coarse sea salt, some sesame seeds, or a few crushed fennel seeds. Cook in a preheated oven, 425°F, for about 15 minutes until well risen and golden. Cut into wedges and serve on top of your casserole.

CHEAT'S TOAD IN THE HOLE

Buy some ready-made Yorkshire puddings, reheat in the oven, and fill with Sausages with Caramelized Onion Gravy (see pages 70–71), adding extra steamed vegetables if you desire.

BREAD

Slice and arrange pieces of oven-baked or toasted ready-made garlic bread on the casserole just before serving or, if you have time, make some garlic croutes by frying sliced or diced bread in olive oil and butter and then rubbing it with a cut garlic clove. Alternatively, toast some sliced ciabatta or French bread and spread it with homemade herb butter.

Buy some spiced tortilla chips and arrange them on top of chilied ground beef, chicken, or lamb. Add a sprinkling of grated cheese and some torn cilantro leaves. Spoon a cooked beef casserole onto warmed tortilla wraps, add a little grated cheese or sour cream, roll them up and serve with a crunchy salad. Or spoon the casserole into crisp taco shells and top in the same way.

Livening up fruit compote

Make a simple fruit compote, such as Winter Berry Compote (see page 214), and liven it up in one of the following ways.

Spoon the fruit compote into a pie dish, top with a basic crumble mix flavored with a little grated orange zest or grated marzipan and bake in the oven until golden.

Line the base of an ovenproof dish with trifle sponge cakes drizzled with a little sherry. Add the fruit compote, a layer of canned custard, and spoonfuls of meringue. Bake in a preheated oven, 350°F, for 15–20 minutes until the meringue is golden and the trifle is hot throughout.

Top the fruit with spoonfuls of thick yogurt flavored with 1–2 tablespoons lemon curd or a drizzle of honey or maple syrup.

Dip some sliced bread into 2 eggs beaten with 2 tablespoons milk, fry in a little butter until golden, then spoon the fruit on top and dust with confectioners' sugar and a little ground cinnamon.

Spoon the compote over reheated ready-made pancakes or toasted waffles. Top with spoonfuls of thick cream or scoops of vanilla ice cream and a drizzle of maple syrup. Spoon the cooled compote over a baked pavlova topped with whipped cream or mini meringue nests.

Caring for your slow cooker

Because a slow cooker heats food to a lower temperature than a conventional oven, cleaning is child's play: there are no burned-on splashes to deal with. To get rid of more stubborn marks, fill the slow cooker pot with warm, soapy water and allow it to soak. Use a soft cloth to wipe the inside and outside of the housing with a cream or stainless steel cleaner, depending on its finish. Never immerse the housing in water, and always make sure it is turned off before cleaning. Some, but not all, slow cooker pots are dishwasher safe, so check with your instruction manual.

Don't forget

* Some slow cookers need to be preheated before use.
* Meat, poultry, fish, and dairy products must be completely defrosted before they are added to the slow cooker.
* Always add hot liquid to the pot before cooking.
* Foods will not brown in a slow cooker, so either fry ingredients first or brown the top of the finished dish by removing the slow cooker pot from the housing and browning the top under the broiler.
* Don't lift the lid in the first hour of cooking while the slow cooker is heating up to a safe and optimal temperature.
* As the slow cooker heats up it forms a water seal just beneath the lid. Every time you lift the lid you break that seal and add an extra 20 minutes to the cooking time.
* The outside of the slow cooker housing gets hot when in use.
* Don't leave cooked dishes to cool down in the slow cooker when it is turned off.
* Never reheat already cooked foods in a slow cooker.

Soups

There's something comforting about a big bowl of warming soup on a cold day. They are also useful if members of your family come in at different times—everyone can just ladle out a bowlful as they need it. Soup served with a chunk of crusty bread is the ultimate TV dinner.

*V*egetable broth with
mini bacon dumplings

3 tablespoons butter

1 leek, sliced; white and green parts kept separate

1 cup diced rutabaga

1 cup diced parsnip

1 cup diced carrot

1 celery stick, sliced

¼ cup pearl barley

4 cups boiling vegetable or chicken stock

2–3 stems of sage

1 teaspoon English mustard

salt and pepper

DUMPLINGS

¾ cup self-rising flour

⅓ cup shredded vegetable suet

2 slices bacon, finely diced

about 3 tablespoons water

Preheat the slow cooker if necessary; see the manufacturer's handbook. Heat the butter in a skillet, add the white sliced leek and fry for 2–3 minutes until softened. Stir in the root vegetables and celery and fry for 4–5 minutes.

Add the pearl barley to the slow cooker pot. Then add the fried vegetables, the boiling stock, and the sage. Stir in the mustard and a little salt and pepper. Cover with the lid and cook on low for 8–10 hours until the vegetables and barley are tender.

Make the dumplings. Put the flour, suet, and bacon in a bowl with a little salt and pepper. Mix together, then gradually mix in enough water to make a soft but not sticky dough. Knead lightly on a lightly floured surface, then cut into 12 pieces. Roll into balls.

Stir the remaining green leek slices into the soup, add the dumplings, spacing them slightly apart, then replace the lid and cook on low for 45–60 minutes until light and fluffy. Ladle into bowls and serve.

Adapt this soup to use whatever winter vegetables you have, remembering to cut them into dice or cubes about ¾ inch in size so they will cook evenly in the time. If you don't have a leek you could use an onion.

Smoked haddock
& bacon chowder

2 tablespoons butter

1 onion, finely chopped

10 oz potatoes, cut into small dice

4 slices bacon, diced

3 cups boiling fish stock

1 corn ear, leaves stripped and
kernels cut away from the core,
or ¾ cup frozen corn (thawed)

1 bay leaf

1 lb smoked haddock, skinned

⅔ cup heavy cream

salt and pepper

chopped parsley, to garnish

Preheat the slow cooker if necessary; see the manufacturer's handbook. Heat the butter in a skillet, add the onion, potatoes, and bacon and fry gently, stirring, until just beginning to brown.

Add to the slow cooker pot. Pour over the boiling stock, then add the corn, bay leaf, and a little salt and pepper. Cover with the lid and cook on high for 2–3 hours or until the potatoes are tender.

Add the fish and press it just beneath the surface of the stock, cutting the pieces in half if needed. Replace the lid and cook for 30 minutes until the fish breaks into flakes when pressed with a knife.

Lift the fish onto a plate with a slotted spoon and break it into flakes with a knife and fork, checking for and removing any bones. Stir the cream into the soup, then return the fish. Sprinkle with parsley and serve.

This soup cooks quickly, so make sure that you chop the onion finely and cut the potatoes evenly into small dice, about ½ inch in size, so that they will both be cooked at the same time.

PREPARATION TIME **20 minutes**

COOKING TEMPERATURE **low**

COOKING TIME **6–8 hours**

SERVES **4**

Tomato, lentil,
& eggplant soup

3–4 tablespoons olive oil, plus extra
to garnish (optional)

1 eggplant, sliced

1 onion, chopped

2 garlic cloves, finely chopped

1/2 teaspoon smoked paprika
(pimenton)

1 teaspoon ground cumin

1/2 cup red lentils

13 oz can chopped tomatoes

3 cups boiling vegetable stock

salt and pepper

chopped cilantro, to garnish

toasted sliced ciabatta bread,
to serve (optional)

Preheat the slow cooker if necessary; see the manufacturer's handbook. Heat 1 tablespoon oil in a skillet, add as many eggplant slices as you can to cover the base of the pan and fry them until softened and golden on both sides.

Transfer the fried eggplant to a plate, add 1–2 more tablespoons of oil and cook the rest of the eggplant. Add to the plate with the other fried eggplant slices.

Add the remaining oil to the pan and fry the onion for 5 minutes until softened. Stir in the garlic, paprika, and cumin and cook for 1 minute. Mix in the lentils and tomatoes. Add a little salt and pepper, then bring to a boil. Pour the mixture into the slow cooker pot and stir in the boiling stock.

Cover with the lid and cook on low for 6–8 hours. Serve the soup as it is or puree it with a stick blender if you prefer. Ladle into bowls, drizzle with a little extra olive oil, sprinkle with cilantro, and serve with toasted sliced ciabatta bread.

If you have a stick blender use it to puree the soup while it is still in the slow cooker pot: it's quick, easy, and saves on dish washing. Alternatively, leave the soup chunky and top it with crispy snipped bacon or dry-fried pancetta slices.

PREPARATION TIME **30 minutes**

COOKING TEMPERATURE **high and low**

COOKING TIME **2¼–3¼ hours**

SERVES **4**

hai broth
with fish dumplings

3¾ cups boiling fish stock

2 teaspoons Thai fish sauce
  (nam pla)

1 tablespoon red Thai curry paste

1 tablespoon soy sauce

1 bunch of scallions, sliced

1 carrot, thinly sliced

2 garlic cloves, finely chopped

1 bunch of asparagus, trimmed and
  stems cut into 4

2 bok choy, thickly sliced, or
  7 oz Swiss chard

DUMPLINGS

¾ cup cilantro leaves

1½ inches fresh ginger root, peeled
  and sliced

13 oz cod, skinned

1 tablespoon cornstarch

1 egg white

Preheat the slow cooker if necessary; see the manufacturer's handbook. Pour the boiling fish stock into the slow cooker pot, add the fish sauce, curry paste, and soy sauce. Add half the scallions, the carrots, and garlic, cover with the lid and cook on high, while making dumplings.

Put the rest of the scallions into a food processor with the cilantro and ginger and chop finely. Add the cod, cornstarch, and egg white and process until the fish is finely chopped.

Shape the mixture into 12 balls with wetted hands, then drop the dumplings into the slow cooker. Cover with the lid and cook on low for 2–3 hours.

Just before serving add the asparagus and bok choy to the broth. Replace the lid and cook for 15 minutes until just tender. Ladle into bowls.

If you are feeling very hungry cook 4 oz dried egg noodles in a saucepan of boiling water, drain, and place spoonfuls in the serving bowls before ladling the soup and dumplings on top.

PREPARATION TIME **20 minutes**

COOKING TEMPERATURE **low and high**

COOKING TIME **4–5 hours**

SERVES **4**

Cheesy cauliflower soup

2 tablespoons butter

1 tablespoon olive oil

1 onion, chopped

1 small baking potato, about 5 oz, cut into small dice

1 cauliflower, trimmed and cut into florets (about 1½ cups when prepared)

2½ cups vegetable stock

1 teaspoon English mustard

3 teaspoons Worcestershire sauce

½ cup grated Parmesan or aged cheddar cheese

¾ cup milk

a little grated nutmeg

⅔ cup heavy cream

salt and pepper

croutons, to serve (optional)

Preheat the slow cooker if necessary; see the manufacturer's handbook. Heat the butter and oil in a skillet, add the onion and potato and fry for 5 minutes or until softened but not browned. Mix in the cauliflower, stock, mustard, Worcestershire sauce, and cheese. Season with a little salt and pepper and bring to a boil.

Pour into the slow cooker pot, cover with the lid, and cook on low for 4–5 hours until the vegetables are tender.

Puree the soup with a stick blender while it is still in the slow cooker or transfer it to a blender and blend until smooth. Return the soup to the slow cooker pot. Stir in the milk, replace the lid, and cook on high for 15 minutes until reheated. Stir and add nutmeg to taste.

Ladle into bowls, swirl cream over the top and sprinkle with a little extra nutmeg or some croutons, or both if desired.

PREPARATION TIME **25 minutes**

COOKING TEMPERATURE **low**

COOKING TIME **6¼–8¼ hours**

SERVES **4**

*C*arrot, orange, & fennel soup

2 tablespoons butter

1 tablespoon sunflower oil

1 large onion, chopped

1 teaspoon fennel seeds,
    roughly crushed

1¼ lb carrots, diced

grated zest and juice of 1 orange

4 cups vegetable stock

salt and pepper

TO SERVE

8 tablespoons heavy cream

handful of croutons

Preheat the slow cooker if necessary; see the manufacturer's handbook. Heat the butter and oil in a skillet, add the onion and fry, stirring, for 5 minutes or until the onion is just beginning to soften.

Stir in the fennel seeds and cook for 1 minute to release the flavor. Mix in the carrots, fry for 2 more minutes, then stir in the orange zest and juice. Tip into the slow cooker pot.

Bring the stock to a boil in the skillet, add salt and pepper, then pour into the slow cooker pot. Cover with the lid and cook on low for 6–8 hours or until the carrots are tender.

Transfer to a blender and puree, in batches if necessary, until smooth, then return to the slow cooker pot. Alternatively, puree the soup still in the slow cooker pot with a stick blender. Reheat if necessary in the covered slow cooker pot for 15 minutes. Ladle the soup into bowls and serve with a drizzle of cream and croutons.

PREPARATION TIME **15 minutes**

COOKING TEMPERATURE **high**

COOKING TIME **3¼ hours–4½ hours**

SERVES **4**

*C*rab gumbo

1 tablespoon sunflower oil

1 onion, finely chopped

1 garlic clove, chopped

2 celery sticks, sliced

1 carrot, cut into small dice

13 oz can chopped tomatoes

2½ cups fish stock

¼ cup easy-cook white rice

1 bay leaf

2 stems of thyme

¼ teaspoon dried red pepper flakes

3 oz okra, stalks trimmed and sliced

1¾ oz can dressed crab meat

salt and pepper

TO SERVE

5¾ oz can white crab meat
    (optional)

crusty bread

Preheat the slow cooker if necessary; see the manufacturer's handbook. Heat the oil in a skillet, add the onion and fry for 5 minutes until softened. Stir in the garlic, celery, and carrot, then mix in the tomatoes, stock, rice, herbs, and pepper flakes. Season with a little salt and pepper and bring to a boil.

Pour into the slow cooker pot, cover with the lid, and cook on high for 3–4 hours until the vegetables and rice are tender.

Stir the soup, then add the okra and dressed crab. Replace the lid and cook for 20–30 minutes. Ladle into bowls, top with the flaked white crab meat, if desired, and serve with warm crusty bread.

If you can't get any okra add the same weight of green beans. If you desire, you can also add diced red or orange sweet peppers with the celery or a handful of shrimp (thawed if frozen) along with the dressed crab at the end.

PREPARATION TIME **20 minutes**

COOKING TEMPERATURE **low**

COOKING TIME **6–8 hours**

SERVES **4**

Chunky chickpea
& chorizo soup

2 tablespoons olive oil

1 onion, chopped

2 garlic cloves, finely chopped

5 oz chorizo, skinned and diced

3/4 teaspoon smoked paprika
   (pimenton)

2–3 stems of thyme

4 cups chicken stock

1 tablespoon tomato paste

2 cups diced sweet potatoes

13 1/2 oz can chickpeas, drained

salt and pepper

chopped parsley or extra thyme
   leaves, to garnish

Preheat the slow cooker if necessary; see the manufacturer's handbook. Heat the oil in a skillet, add the onion and fry, stirring, for 5 minutes or until just beginning to turn golden.

Stir in the garlic and chorizo and cook for 2 minutes. Mix in the paprika, add the thyme, stock, and tomato paste and bring to a boil, stirring, then add a little salt and pepper.

Add the sweet potatoes and chickpeas to the slow cooker pot and pour over the hot stock mixture. Cover with the lid and cook on low for 6–8 hours until the sweet potatoes are tender.

Ladle into bowls, sprinkle with a little chopped parsley or extra thyme and serve with warm pita breads, if desired.

Chicken & noodle broth

1 chicken carcass

1 onion, cut into wedges

2 carrots, sliced

2 celery sticks, sliced

1 bouquet garni

5 cups boiling water

3 oz vermicelli pasta

4 tablespoons chopped parsley

salt and pepper

bread, to serve (optional)

Preheat the slow cooker if necessary; see the manufacturer's handbook. Put the chicken carcass into the slow cooker pot, breaking it into 2 pieces if necessary to make it fit. Add the onion, carrots, celery, and bouquet garni.

Pour over the boiling water and add a little salt and pepper. Cover with the lid and cook on high for 5–7 hours.

Strain the soup through a large strainer, then quickly pour the hot liquid back into the slow cooker pot. Take any meat off the carcass and add to the pot. Taste and adjust the seasoning if needed. Add the pasta, cover with the lid, and cook on high for 20–30 minutes or until the pasta is just cooked.

Sprinkle with parsley and ladle into deep bowls. Serve with warm bread, if desired.

Light bites

Here are some smaller snacks and
quick fixes for breakfast, lunch,
and tea. Some of the breakfasts
can be put on before you go to bed
so that you have a hot breakfast
waiting for you when you get up
in the morning.

PREPARATION TIME **5 minutes**

COOKING TEMPERATURE **low**

COOKING TIME **8–10 hours or overnight**

SERVES **4**

$\mathcal{B}$reakfast compote

1 breakfast tea teabag

2½ cups boiling water

1 cup pitted prunes

1 cup dried figs

⅓ cup superfine sugar

1 teaspoon vanilla extract

pared rind of ½ orange

TO SERVE

plain yogurt

granola

Preheat the slow cooker if necessary; see the manufacturer's handbook. Put the teabag into a pitcher or teapot, add the boiling water and allow to infuse for 2–3 minutes. Remove the teabag and pour the tea into the slow cooker pot.

Add the whole prunes and figs, the sugar, and vanilla extract to the hot tea, sprinkle with the orange rind and mix together. Cover with the lid and cook on low for 8–10 hours or overnight.

Serve hot with spoonfuls of plain yogurt and a sprinkling of granola.

This breakfast treat also tastes delicious made with an Earl Grey tea bag to add a tang of bergamot. It can also be served warm as a dessert with cream-filled meringues or scoops of ice cream.

*E*ggs en cocotte
with smoked salmon

2 tablespoons butter

4 eggs

4 tablespoons heavy cream

2 teaspoons chopped chives

1 teaspoon chopped tarragon

salt and pepper

TO SERVE

7 oz smoked salmon, sliced

4 lemon wedges

4 slices toast

Preheat the slow cooker if necessary; see the manufacturer's handbook. Liberally butter the inside of 4 x ¾ cup heatproof china ramekin dishes and break an egg into each one.

Drizzle the cream over the eggs and sprinkle with the herbs and a little salt and pepper. Transfer the ramekins to the slow cooker pot and pour boiling water into the pot to come halfway up the sides of the ramekins.

Cover with the lid (there is no need to cover the dishes with foil) and cook on high for 40–45 minutes or until the egg whites are set but the yolks are still slightly soft.

Lift the dishes carefully out of the slow cooker pot with a dishtowel, transfer to plates and serve with smoked salmon, lemon wedges, and triangles of toast.

Try ringing the changes and serve the eggs with sliced ham or broiled bacon and toasted English muffins. Alternatively you could serve them with mixed salad leaves that have been tossed in a mustard dressing.

$\mathscr{S}$piced banana oatmeal

2½ cups boiling water

1¼ cups whole ultrapasteurized milk

1½ cups rolled oats

2 bananas

4 tablespoons light or dark brown sugar

¼ teaspoon ground cinnamon

Preheat the slow cooker if necessary; see the manufacturer's handbook. Pour the boiling water and milk into the slow cooker pot, then stir in the oats.

Cover with the lid and cook on low for 1 hour for runny oatmeal or 2 hours for thick oatmeal.

Spoon into bowls, slice the bananas, and divide among the bowls. Mix together the sugar and cinnamon and sprinkle over the top. Serve immediately.

This recipe is perfect for those who like to go for a run or walk the dogs before breakfast. Put the oatmeal on before you go out and you will have a delicious and warming breakfast ready and waiting when you get back.

PREPARATION TIME **20 minutes**

COOKING TEMPERATURE **low**

COOKING TIME **9–10 hours or overnight**

SERVES **4**

$\mathcal{B}$ig breakfast bonanza

1 tablespoon sunflower oil

12 herby chipolata sausages, about 13 oz in total

1 onion, thinly sliced

1 lb potatoes, peeled and cut into 1 inch chunks

12 oz tomatoes, roughly chopped

4 oz blood sausage, peeled and cut into chunks

1 cup vegetable stock

2 tablespoons Worcestershire sauce

1 teaspoon English mustard

2–3 stems of thyme, plus extra to garnish

salt and pepper

TO SERVE

slices of white bread (optional)

4 poached eggs (optional)

Preheat the slow cooker if necessary; see the manufacturer's handbook. Heat the oil in a skillet, add the sausages and brown on one side, turn and add the onion. Fry, turning the sausages and stirring the onions until the sausages are browned but not cooked.

Add the potatoes, tomatoes, and blood sausage to the slow cooker pot. Lift the sausages and onion from the pan with a slotted spoon and transfer them to the slow cooker pot. Pour off the excess fat, then add the stock, Worcestershire sauce, and mustard to the pan. Tear the leaves from the thyme stems and add to pan with some salt and pepper.

Bring the sauce to a boil and pour over the sausages. Press the potatoes down so that the liquid covers them. Cover with the lid and cook on low for 9–10 hours or overnight.

Stir the dish before serving and garnish with extra thyme leaves. Serve with slices of white bread or a poached egg, if desired.

PREPARATION TIME **15 minutes**

COOKING TEMPERATURE **low**

COOKING TIME **9–10 hours or overnight**

SERVES **4**

Easy sausage & beans

1 tablespoon sunflower oil

1 onion, chopped

1/2 teaspoon smoked paprika (pimenton)

2 x 13 1/2 oz cans baked beans

2 teaspoons grainy mustard

2 tablespoons Worcestershire sauce

6 tablespoons vegetable stock

2 tomatoes, roughly chopped

1/2 red bell pepper, cored, seeded, and diced

12 oz chilled frankfurters, thickly sliced

salt and pepper

buttered toast, to serve

Preheat the slow cooker if necessary; see the manufacturer's handbook. Heat the oil in a skillet, add the onion and fry, stirring, for 5 minutes or until softened and just beginning to turn golden.

Stir in the paprika and cook for 1 minute, then mix in the beans, mustard, Worcestershire sauce, and stock. Bring to a boil, then stir in the tomatoes, red pepper, and a little salt and pepper.

Add the frankfurters to the slow cooker pot and tip the baked bean mixture over the top. Cover with the lid and cook on low for 9–10 hours or overnight.

Stir well, then spoon into shallow bowls and serve with the buttered toast.

Any leftovers can be reheated in a saucepan or in the microwave and served with rice. Alternatively you could try them spooned over a crispy baked potato served straight from the oven.

Zucchini &
fava bean frittata

3 tablespoons butter

4 scallions, sliced

1 zucchini, about 7 oz, thinly sliced

²/₃ cup podded fresh fava beans

6 eggs

1 cup full-fat sour cream

2 teaspoons chopped tarragon

2 tablespoons chopped parsley

salt and pepper

TO SERVE

salad

Beet Chutney (optional)

Preheat the slow cooker if necessary; see the manufacturer's handbook. Put the butter, onions, and zucchini into a bowl and cook in the microwave for 2½–3 minutes on full power until the butter has melted.

Line the slow cooker pot with a piece of nonstick parchment paper, tip in the zucchini and butter mix, then add the fava beans. Fork together the eggs, sour cream, herbs, and a little salt and pepper in the bowl then pour into the slow cooker pot.

Cover with the lid and cook the frittata on high for 1½–2 hours until set in the middle. Loosen the edge with a round-bladed knife, take the slow cooker pot out of the machine with oven mitts, then cover with a large plate, invert the pot onto the plate, then remove. Peel off the lining paper and cut the frittata into wedges. Serve with salad and spoonfuls of Beet Chutney (see pages 218–219), if desired.

This light, summery lunch dish is ideal for anyone who is short on time, because nothing needs to be fried on the stovetop first. You can use frozen beans, but make sure they are thawed before you add them to the slow cooker pot.

PREPARATION TIME **15 minutes**

COOKING TEMPERATURE **high**

COOKING TIME **2–3 hours**

SERVES **4**

Chilied corn

1 tablespoon sunflower oil

1 onion, finely chopped

1 orange bell pepper, cored, seeded, and diced

³/₄ cup frozen corn, thawed

1 garlic clove, finely chopped

large pinch (or more to taste) dried red pepper flakes

¹/₂ teaspoon ground cumin

1 teaspoon ground coriander

13¹/₂ oz can mixed beans

13 oz can chopped tomatoes

²/₃ cup vegetable stock

2 teaspoons brown sugar

salt and pepper

TO SERVE

8 tablespoons sour cream

grated cheddar cheese

4 baked potatoes (optional)

Preheat the slow cooker if necessary; see the manufacturer's handbook. Heat the oil in a skillet, add the onion and fry for 5 minutes, stirring, until softened. Stir in the pepper, corn, garlic, and spices, cook for 1 minute, then add the beans, tomatoes, stock, and sugar. Add a little salt and pepper, mix together and bring to a boil.

Pour the mixture into the slow cooker pot, cover with the lid, and cook on high for 2–3 hours.

Serve the chili with sour cream and cheese, or spooned on top of baked potatoes.

You could add 8 oz extra lean ground beef when you are frying the onion. Increase the cooking time to 3–4 hours. An alternative to serving with baked potatoes is to top the chili with tortilla chips, sour cream, and grated cheese.

$\mathscr{M}$editerranean
roasted vegetable terrine

12 oz zucchini, thinly sliced

1 red bell pepper, quartered, seeded, and cored

1 orange bell pepper, quartered, seeded, and cored

2 tablespoons olive oil

1 garlic clove, finely chopped

2 eggs

2/3 cup whole milk

1/4 cup grated Parmesan cheese

3 tablespoons chopped basil

salt and pepper

salad, to serve (optional)

Preheat the slow cooker if necessary; see the manufacturer's handbook. Line the broiler rack with foil. Arrange all the vegetables on the foil in a single layer, with the peppers skin side up. Drizzle with the oil and sprinkle with the garlic and salt and pepper.

Broil the vegetables for 10 minutes or until softened and browned. Transfer the zucchini slices to a plate and wrap the peppers in the foil. Allow to stand for 5 minutes to loosen the skins.

In a bowl beat together the eggs, milk, Parmesan, basil, and a little salt and pepper. Lightly oil a 1 lb loaf pan and line the base and 2 long sides with a piece of nonstick parchment paper.

Unwrap the peppers, peel away the skins with a small, sharp knife and add any juices in the foil to the custard. Arrange one-third of the zucchini slices over the base of the pan or until covered. Spoon in a little of the basil custard, then add the peppers and a little more custard. Repeat, ending with a layer of zucchini and custard. Cover the top loosely with oiled foil and put in the slow cooker pot.

Pour boiling water into the slow cooker to come halfway up the sides of the pan. Cover with the lid and cook on high for 2–3 hours or until the custard is set. Take the pan out of the slow cooker with a dishtowel and allow to cool.

Loosen the edge of the terrine with a round-bladed knife. Invert the pan onto a cutting board and peel away the paper. Cut the terrine into slices and serve with salad, if desired.

PREPARATION TIME **30 minutes**

COOKING TEMPERATURE **high**

COOKING TIME **5–6 hours**

SERVES **4**

$\mathcal{D}$uck, pork, &
apple rillettes

2 duck legs

1 lb pork belly slices, halved

1 onion, cut into wedges

1 sharp dessert apple, such as Granny
   Smith, peeled, cored, and thickly
   sliced

2–3 sprigs of thyme

1 cup chicken stock

⅔ cup hard cider

salt and pepper

TO SERVE

crusty bread

radishes

pickled shallots (optional)

Preheat the slow cooker if necessary; see the manufacturer's handbook. Put the duck and pork belly into the base of the slow cooker pot. Tuck the onion and apple between the pieces of meat and add the thyme.

Pour the stock and cider into a saucepan, add plenty of salt and pepper and bring to a boil.

Pour the hot liquid into the slow cooker pot, cover with the lid, and cook on high for 5–6 hours until the duck and pork are tender.

Allow to cool for 30 minutes, then lift the meat out of the slow cooker pot with a slotted spoon and transfer it to a large plate. Peel away the duck skin and remove the bones. Shred the meat into small pieces with a knife and fork. Discard the thyme sprigs. Scoop out the apple and onion with a slotted spoon and finely chop. Mix the apple and onion with the meat, then taste and add salt and pepper if necessary.

Pack the chopped meat mix into 4 individual dishes or small "le parfait" jars and press down firmly. Spoon over the juices still remaining in the slow cooker pot to cover and seal the meat, then allow to cool. Transfer to the refrigerator and chill well. When the fat has solidified on the top, cover each dish with a lid or plastic wrap. They can be kept in the refrigerator for up to 1 week.

Serve the rillettes with warm crusty bread, a few radishes, and pickled shallots, if desired.

Turkey, cranberry,
& orange meatloaf

$3^3/4$ oz package dried orange and cranberry stuffing mix

$1/4$ cup dried cranberries

1 tablespoon sunflower oil

1 onion, finely chopped

1 lb skinless turkey breast steaks

7 oz bacon

1 egg, beaten

salt and pepper

TO SERVE

salad

cranberry sauce (optional)

Beet Chutney (optional)

Put the stuffing mix in a bowl, add the cranberries and mix with boiling water as the instructions on the stuffing package direct.

Heat the oil in a skillet, add the onion, and fry for 5 minutes, stirring, until softened. Set aside. Finely chop the turkey slices in a food processor or pass through a coarse grinder.

Meanwhile, preheat the slow cooker if necessary; see the manufacturer's handbook. Take a soufflé dish that is $5^1/2$ inches in diameter and $3^1/2$ inches high and line the base with waxed or nonstick parchment paper. Stretch each slice of bacon with the flat of a large cook's knife until half as long again, and use about three-quarters of the slices to line the base and sides of the dish, trimming to fit as necessary.

Mix the stuffing with the fried onion, chopped turkey, and egg. Season well and spoon into the bacon-lined dish. Press flat and cover with the remaining slices of bacon.

Cover the dish with foil and lower into the slow cooker pot. Pour boiling water into the pot to come halfway up the sides of the dish, then add the lid and cook on high for 5–6 hours or until the juices run clear when the center of the meatloaf is pierced with a small knife.

Lift the dish out of the slow cooker with oven mitts. Allow the meatloaf to cool in the dish, then chill in the refrigerator overnight until firm. Loosen the edge with a round-bladed knife, turn out, and peel off the lining paper. Cut into thick slices and serve with salad and spoonfuls of cranberry sauce or Beet Chutney (see pages 218–219), if desired.

PREPARATION TIME **20 minutes**

COOKING TEMPERATURE **low**

COOKING TIME **9–10 hours**

or overnight

SERVES **4**

Potato, apple, & bacon hotpot

1½ lb potatoes, thinly sliced

2 tablespoons butter

1 tablespoon sunflower oil

2 onions, roughly chopped

8 oz bacon, diced

1 dessert apple, cored and sliced

2 tablespoons all-purpose flour

1¾ cups chicken stock

2 teaspoons English mustard

2 bay leaves

½ cup grated cheddar cheese

salt and pepper

broiled tomato halves, to serve (optional)

Preheat the slow cooker if necessary; see the manufacturer's handbook. Bring a large saucepan of water to a boil, add the potatoes, cook for 3 minutes, then drain.

Heat the butter and oil in a skillet, add the onions and bacon and fry, stirring, for 5 minutes or until just beginning to turn golden. Stir in the apple and flour and season the mixture well with salt and pepper.

Layer the potatoes and the onion mixture in the slow cooker pot, ending with a layer of potatoes. Add the stock and mustard to the skillet, bring to a boil, then pour into the slow cooker pot. And add the bay leaves. Cover with the lid and cook on low for 9–10 hours.

Sprinkle the top of the potatoes with the cheese, lift the pot out of the housing using oven mitts and brown under a preheated hot broiler. Spoon into shallow bowls and serve with broiled tomato halves, if desired.

*B*eery cheese fondue

1 tablespoon butter

2 shallots or ½ small onion, finely chopped

1 garlic clove, finely chopped

3 teaspoons cornstarch

¾ cup blond beer

7 oz Gruyère cheese (rind removed), grated

6 oz Emmental cheese (rind removed), grated

grated nutmeg

salt and pepper

TO SERVE

½ whole-wheat French stick, cubed

2 celery sticks, cut into short lengths

8 small pickled onions, drained and halved

1 bunch of radishes, tops trimmed

1 red bell pepper, cored, seeded, and cubed

2 endive, leaves separated

Preheat the slow cooker if necessary; see the manufacturer's handbook. Butter the inside of the slow cooker pot, then add the shallots or onion and garlic.

Put the cornstarch in a small bowl, add a little of the beer, and mix to make a smooth paste. Blend in the remaining beer. Add to the slow cooker with both cheeses, a little nutmeg, and some salt and pepper.

Stir together, cover with the lid, and cook on high for 40–60 minutes, beating once during cooking. Beat again and serve with the dippers arranged on a serving plate, with long fondue or ordinary forks for dunking the dippers into the fondue.

Everyday suppers

Do you sometimes feel that you add the same ingredients to your supermarket cart every week as if you are on automatic pilot? Ring the changes with some tasty twists to old favorites and encourage the children to try something new too.

Cidered pork
with sage dumplings

1 tablespoon sunflower oil

1¹/₂ lb pork shoulder steaks, cubed
and any fat discarded

1 leek, thinly sliced; white and green
parts kept separate

2 tablespoons all-purpose flour

1¹/₄ cups hard cider

1¹/₄ cups chicken stock

1¹/₄ cups diced carrot

1 dessert apple, cored and diced

2–3 stems of sage

salt and pepper

DUMPLINGS

1¹/₄ cups self-rising flour

³/₄ cup vegetable suet

1 tablespoon chopped sage

2 tablespoons chopped parsley

5–7 tablespoons water

Preheat the slow cooker if necessary; see the manufacturer's handbook. Heat the oil in a skillet, add the pork a few pieces at a time until all the pieces are in the pan, then fry over a high heat until lightly browned. Lift the pork out of the pan with a slotted spoon and transfer it to the slow cooker pot.

Add the white leek slices to the pan and fry for 2–3 minutes or until softened. Stir in the flour, then gradually mix in the cider and stock. Add the carrot, apple, sage, and some salt and pepper. Bring to a boil, stirring continuously.

Pour the mixture into the slow cooker pot, cover with the lid, and cook on low for 8–10 hours or until the pork is tender.

Make the dumplings. Put the flour, suet, herbs, and a little salt and pepper into a bowl, mix together, then gradually stir in enough water to make a soft but not sticky dough. Cut into 12 pieces and roll them into balls with floured hands.

Stir the green leek slices into the casserole and arrange the dumplings on the top. Cover with the lid and cook, still on low, for 1 hour until they are well risen. Spoon the stew into shallow bowls to serve.

PREPARATION TIME **15 minutes**

COOKING TEMPERATURE **low**

COOKING TIME **8¼–10¼ hours**

SERVES **4**

Mustard chicken &
bacon casserole

1 tablespoon butter

1 tablespoon sunflower oil

4 chicken thighs and 4 chicken
    drumstick joints

4 slices bacon, diced

13 oz leeks, thinly sliced; white and
    green parts kept separate

2 tablespoons all-purpose flour

2½ cups chicken stock

3 teaspoons grainy mustard

salt and pepper

mashed potatoes, to serve (optional)

Preheat the slow cooker if necessary; see the manufacturer's handbook. Heat the butter and oil in a skillet, add the chicken joints, and fry over a high heat until browned on all sides. Remove from the pan with a slotted spoon and transfer to the slow cooker pot.

Add the bacon and white leek slices to the skillet and fry, stirring, for 5 minutes or until just beginning to turn golden. Stir in the flour, then gradually mix in the stock, mustard, and a little salt and pepper. Bring to a boil. Pour into the slow cooker pot, cover with the lid, and cook on low for 8–10 hours.

Add the green leek slices and stir into the sauce. Replace the lid and cook, still on low, for 15 minutes or until the green leeks are just softened. Spoon the casserole into shallow serving bowls and serve with mashed potatoes, if desired.

For a different take on this dish, replace a quarter of the chicken stock with ⅔ cup red wine or hard cider, omit the leeks and mustard and add shallots and a bouquet garni. Or you could try adding a few pitted prunes or dried chestnuts to the casserole.

Moussaka

4 tablespoons olive oil

1 large eggplant, thinly sliced

1 lb ground lamb

1 onion, chopped

2 garlic cloves, finely chopped

1 tablespoon all-purpose flour

13 oz can chopped tomatoes

¾ cup lamb stock

1 teaspoon ground cinnamon

¼ teaspoon grated nutmeg

1 tablespoon tomato paste

salt and pepper

salad, to serve (optional)

TOPPING

3 eggs

1 cup plain yogurt

3 oz feta cheese, grated

pinch of grated nutmeg

Preheat the slow cooker if necessary; see the manufacturer's handbook. Heat half the oil in a skillet and fry the eggplant slices in batches, adding more oil as needed until they have all been fried and are softened and lightly browned on both sides. Drain and transfer to a plate.

Add the ground lamb and onion to the skillet and dry-fry, stirring and breaking up the lamb, until evenly browned. Stir in the garlic and flour, then mix in the tomatoes, stock, spices, tomato paste, and a little salt and pepper. Bring to a boil, stirring.

Spoon the lamb mixture into the slow cooker pot and arrange the eggplant slices on top, overlapping them to cover the top evenly. Cover with the lid and cook on low for 8–10 hours.

Make the custard topping. Mix together the eggs, yogurt, feta, and nutmeg. Spoon the mixture over the eggplant, replace the lid, and cook, still on low, for ¾–1¼ hours or until set. Lift the pot out of the housing using oven mitts and brown under a hot broiler. Serve with salad.

Although not very Greek, this dish can be served without the custard topping, adding mashed potatoes flavored with yogurt or cheddar cheese instead. You could also simply spoon the meaty mixture on top of a dish of rice.

PREPARATION TIME **20 minutes**

COOKING TEMPERATURE **low**

COOKING TIME **5–7 hours**

SERVES **4**

Mackerel with
harissa potatoes

1 lb new potatoes, scrubbed and thickly sliced

1 tablespoon olive oil

1 onion, chopped

$\frac{1}{2}$ red bell pepper, cored, seeded, and diced

$\frac{1}{2}$ yellow bell pepper, cored, seeded, and diced

1 garlic clove, finely chopped

2 teaspoons harissa (Moroccan chili paste)

$\frac{3}{4}$ cup roughly chopped tomatoes

1 tablespoon tomato paste

$1\frac{1}{4}$ cups fish stock

4 small mackerel, each about 10 oz, gutted and heads removed

salt and pepper

pita breads, to serve (optional)

Preheat the slow cooker if necessary; see the manufacturer's handbook. Bring a saucepan of water to a boil, add the potatoes, and cook for 4–5 minutes or until almost tender. Drain and reserve.

Heat the oil in a skillet, add the onion and fry, stirring, for 5 minutes or until softened and just beginning to turn golden. Stir in the peppers and garlic and fry for 2–3 minutes. Mix in the harissa, tomatoes, tomato paste, stock, and a little salt and pepper and bring to a boil.

Tip the potatoes into the slow cooker pot. Rinse the fish well, drain, and arrange in a single layer on top of the potatoes, then cover with the hot tomato mixture. Cover with the lid and cook on low for 5–7 hours or until the potatoes are tender and the fish flakes when pressed in the center with a small knife.

Spoon into shallow bowls and serve with warmed pita breads, if desired.

Mackerel are surprisingly cheap and are a rich source of omega 3 fatty acids, which are thought to boost brain power and help protect against heart and circulation problems.

$\mathscr{S}$ausages with
caramelized onion gravy

1 tablespoon sunflower oil

8 specialty flavored sausages, such as Sicilian or Toulouse

2 red onions, halved and thinly sliced

2 teaspoons light brown sugar

2 tablespoons all-purpose flour

1¾ cups beef stock

1 tablespoon sun-dried or ordinary tomato paste

1 bay leaf

salt and pepper

TO SERVE

carrots

broccoli

Preheat the slow cooker if necessary; see the manufacturer's handbook. Heat the oil in a skillet, add the sausages and fry over a high heat for 5 minutes, turning until browned on all sides but not cooked through. Drain and transfer to the slow cooker pot.

Add the onions to the skillet and fry over a medium heat for 5 minutes or until softened. Add the sugar and fry, stirring, for 5 more minutes or until the onion slices are caramelized around the edges.

Stir in the flour, then gradually mix in the stock. Add the tomato paste, the bay leaf, and some salt and pepper and bring to a boil, still stirring. Pour over the sausages. Cover with the lid and cook on low for 6–8 hours or until the sausages are cooked through.

Serve the sausages and gravy spooned into reheated ready-made large Yorkshire puddings and accompanied with steamed carrots and broccoli.

If you are opening some beer to drink with the meal, you could reduce the amount of stock to 1½ cups and add a splash of beer at the very end of cooking.

PREPARATION TIME **25 minutes**

COOKING TEMPERATURE **high**

COOKING TIME **5–7 hours**

SERVES **4**

$\mathcal{M}$aple-glazed ribs

$2^{1}/_{2}$ lb pork ribs, rinsed with cold
water and drained

1 onion, quartered

1 carrot, thickly sliced

2 bay leaves

2 tablespoons malt vinegar

1 teaspoon black peppercorns

$^{1}/_{2}$ teaspoon salt

4 cups boiling water

GLAZE

2 teaspoons English mustard

1 teaspoon ground allspice

2 tablespoons tomato paste

2 tablespoons brown sugar

$^{1}/_{2}$ cup maple syrup

COLESLAW

2 carrots, grated

$^{1}/_{4}$ red cabbage, shredded

3 scallions, sliced

$^{1}/_{2}$ cup corn (thawed if frozen)

2 tablespoons mayonnaise

2 tablespoons plain yogurt

Preheat the slow cooker if necessary; see the manufacturer's handbook. Put the pork, onion, carrot, bay leaves, vinegar, peppercorns, salt, and boiling water into the slow cooker pot, cover with the lid, and cook on high for 5–7 hours or until the ribs are tender.

Remove the ribs from the slow cooker with a slotted spoon and transfer to a foil-lined broiler pan. Mix together the ingredients for the glaze with $^{2}/_{3}$ cup hot stock from the slow cooker pot. Spoon the glaze over the ribs, then broil for 10–15 minutes, turning once or twice, until browned and sticky.

Meanwhile, mix together the ingredients for the coleslaw and spoon into 4 small bowls. Place these on dinner plates, then pile the ribs onto the plates to serve.

In the summertime you can barbecue the glaze ribs (minus the stock) over preheated coals, dousing any flames from the juices spitting on the coals with a water sprayer. This will give the sweet and sticky ribs a wonderful smoky flavor.

PREPARATION TIME **20 minutes**

COOKING TEMPERATURE **low**

COOKING TIME **8–10 hours**

SERVES **4**

Gourmet bolognese

1 tablespoon olive oil

1 lb lean ground beef

1 onion, chopped

8 oz chicken livers (thawed if frozen)

2 garlic cloves, finely chopped

2 oz pancetta or bacon, diced

2 cups sliced mushrooms

1 tablespoon all-purpose flour

$^2/_3$ cup red wine

$^2/_3$ cup beef stock

13 oz can chopped tomatoes

2 tablespoons tomato paste

1 bouquet garni

salt and pepper

10 oz tagliatelle

TO SERVE

shaved Parmesan cheese

basil leaves

Preheat the slow cooker if necessary; see the manufacturer's handbook. Heat the oil in a skillet, add the beef and onion and fry, stirring and breaking up the meat with a spoon until it is evenly browned.

Meanwhile, rinse the chicken livers in a strainer, drain and chop roughly, discarding any white cores. Add to the skillet with the garlic, pancetta or bacon, and mushrooms and cook for 2–3 minutes or until the livers are browned.

Stir in the flour, then mix in the wine, stock, tomatoes, tomato paste, bouquet garni, and salt and pepper. Bring to a boil, stirring. Spoon into the slow cooker pot, cover with the lid, and cook on low for 8–10 hours.

Just before serving put the tagliatelle into a saucepan of boiling salted water and cook for 8 minutes or until just tender. Drain and stir into the bolognese. Spoon into shallow bowls and sprinkle with Parmesan shavings and some basil leaves.

Bolognese sauce does not have to be made with ground beef despite what the traditionalists say; try ground lamb or even ground pork for a change. You could also shape the beef and livers into meatballs if preferred.

PREPARATION TIME **15 minutes**

COOKING TEMPERATURE **low**

COOKING TIME **2¼–3¼ hours**

SERVES **4**

Cheesy macaroni
with smoked haddock

7 oz macaroni

1 tablespoon olive oil

1 onion, chopped

¼ cup butter

½ cup all-purpose flour

1¾ cups whole ultrapasteurized milk

1¾ cups fish stock

1¾ cups grated cheddar cheese

¼ teaspoon grated nutmeg

1 lb smoked haddock, skinned and cut into 1 inch cubes

7 oz can corn, drained

2½ cups spinach, rinsed, drained, and roughly torn

salt and pepper

cherry tomatoes, to serve

Preheat the slow cooker if necessary; see the manufacturer's handbook. Tip the macaroni into a bowl, cover with plenty of boiling water, and allow to stand for 10 minutes while you prepare the rest of the dish.

Heat the oil in a saucepan, add the onion and fry gently, stirring, for 5 minutes or until softened. Add the butter and, when melted, stir in the flour. Gradually mix in the milk and bring to a boil, stirring until smooth. Stir in the stock, 1¼ cups of the cheddar, nutmeg, and salt and pepper and bring back to a boil, stirring.

Drain the macaroni and add to the slow cooker pot with the haddock and corn. Pour over the sauce and gently stir together. Cover with the lid and cook on low for 2–3 hours.

Stir the spinach into the macaroni, replace the lid and cook, still on low, for 15 minutes. Lift the pot out of the housing using oven mitts and stir once more. Sprinkle the remaining cheddar over the macaroni, then brown under a preheated hot broiler until the top is golden. Serve with broiled cherry tomatoes on the vine.

$\mathscr{B}$eef hotpot

1 tablespoon sunflower oil

1½ lb braising beef, cubed

1 onion, chopped

2 tablespoons all-purpose flour

2½ cups beef stock

2 tablespoons Worcestershire sauce

1 tablespoon tomato paste

2 teaspoons English mustard

3 sprigs of rosemary

¾ cup diced carrots

¾ cup diced rutabaga

¾ cup diced parsnip

1 lb 6 oz potatoes, thinly sliced

2 tablespoons butter

salt and pepper

Preheat the slow cooker if necessary; see the manufacturer's handbook. Heat the oil in a skillet, add the beef a few pieces at a time until all the meat is in the pan, then fry over a high heat, stirring, until browned. Remove the beef from the pan with a slotted spoon and transfer to the slow cooker pot.

Add the onion to the pan and fry, stirring, for 5 minutes or until softened and just beginning to turn golden. Stir in the flour, then gradually mix in the stock. Add the Worcestershire sauce, tomato paste, mustard, and leaves from 2 sprigs of the rosemary. Season with salt and pepper and bring to a boil, stirring.

Add the diced vegetables to the slow cooker pot. Pour the onion and sauce over them, then cover with the potato slices, arranging them so that they overlap and pressing them down into the stock. Sprinkle with the leaves torn from the remaining stem of rosemary and a little salt and pepper.

Cover with the lid and cook on high for 7–8 hours until the potatoes are tender. Lift the pot out of the housing using oven mitts; dot the potatoes with the butter and brown under a preheated hot broiler, if desired.

PREPARATION TIME **20 minutes**

COOKING TEMPERATURE **low**

COOKING TIME **6–8 hours**

SERVES **4**

Chicken korma

2 tablespoons sunflower oil

8 chicken thighs, about 2 lb in total, skinned, boned, and cubed

2 onions, finely chopped, plus extra to garnish

1–2 green chilies (or to taste), seeded and finely chopped

1 inch fresh ginger root, peeled and finely chopped

5 tablespoons korma curry paste

1 cup coconut cream or coconut milk

1¼ cups chicken stock

2 tablespoons ground almonds

small bunch of cilantro

¾ cup plain yogurt

2 tomatoes, diced

salt and pepper

chapattis, to serve

Preheat the slow cooker if necessary; see the manufacturer's handbook. Heat the oil in a skillet, add the chicken a few pieces at a time until they are all in the pan, then fry, stirring, until golden. Remove the chicken from the pan with a slotted spoon and put it in the slow cooker pot.

Add the onions, chilies, ginger, and curry paste to the pan and fry, stirring, for 2–3 minutes. Pour in the coconut cream or milk, stock, and ground almonds. Tear half the cilantro into pieces and add to the sauce with a little salt and pepper. Bring to a boil, stirring, then spoon over the chicken.

Cover with the lid and cook on low for 6–8 hours.

Stir the korma, then ladle it into bowls, top with spoonfuls of yogurt, the tomatoes, and extra raw onion and the remaining cilantro torn into small pieces. Serve with warm chapattis.

Rather than buying take-out, make the curry, cool, then pack into individual plastic boxes. Freeze and then transfer to the refrigerator the night before you need it or first thing in the morning to defrost. Reheat in the microwave when you get home.

$\mathcal{R}$ancheros pie

1 tablespoon sunflower oil

1 lb ground beef

1 onion, chopped

2 garlic cloves, finely chopped

1 teaspoon cumin seeds, roughly
crushed

1/4–1/2 teaspoon crushed red pepper

1/4 teaspoon ground allspice

2 stems of oregano, roughly chopped

3 tablespoons golden raisins

13 oz can chopped tomatoes

1 cup beef stock

salt and pepper

TOPPING

1 lb sweet potatoes, thinly sliced

2 tablespoons butter

crushed red pepper

Preheat the slow cooker if necessary; see the manufacturer's handbook. Heat the oil in a skillet, add the beef and onion and fry, stirring and breaking up the meat with a wooden spoon, until browned.

Stir in the garlic, spices, oregano, golden raisins, tomatoes, and stock. Add a little salt and pepper and bring to a boil, stirring. Spoon into the slow cooker pot, cover with overlapping slices of sweet potato, dot with butter, and sprinkle with red pepper flakes and a little salt and pepper.

Cover with the lid and cook on low for 7–8 hours until the potato topping is tender. Lift the pot out of the housing using oven mitts and brown under a preheated hot broiler, if desired.

Tuna arrabiata

1 tablespoon olive oil

1 onion, chopped

2 garlic cloves, finely chopped

1 red bell pepper, cored, seeded, and diced

1 teaspoon smoked paprika (pimenton)

1/4–1/2 teaspoon crushed red pepper

13 oz can chopped tomatoes

2/3 cup vegetable or fish stock

7 oz can tuna in water, drained

12 oz spaghetti

salt and pepper

TO SERVE

freshly grated Parmesan cheese

basil leaves

Preheat the slow cooker if necessary; see the manufacturer's handbook. Heat the oil in a skillet, add the onion and fry, stirring, for 5 minutes or until just beginning to turn golden around the edges.

Stir in the garlic, red pepper, paprika, and crushed pepper and cook for 2 minutes. Mix in the tomatoes, stock, and a little salt and pepper. Bring to a boil, then tip into the slow cooker pot. Break the tuna into large pieces and stir into the tomato mixture. Cover with the lid and cook on low for 4–5 hours.

When almost ready to serve, bring a large saucepan of water to a boil, add the spaghetti, and cook for about 8 minutes or until tender. Drain and stir into the tomato sauce. Spoon into shallow bowls and serve sprinkled with grated Parmesan and basil leaves.

PREPARATION TIME **15 minutes**

COOKING TEMPERATURE **low**

COOKING TIME **8–10 hours**

SERVES **4**

*L*amb tagine
with figs & almonds

1 tablespoon olive oil

1½ lb boned rib of lamb, diced,
   or ready-diced lamb

1 onion, sliced

2 garlic cloves, finely chopped

1 inch fresh ginger root, peeled and
   finely chopped

2 tablespoons all-purpose flour

2½ cups lamb stock

1 teaspoon ground cinnamon

2 large pinches of saffron threads

⅓ cup dried figs, stalks trimmed off
   and fruits diced

½ cup toasted slivered almonds

salt and pepper

lemon and chickpea couscous,
   to serve

Preheat the slow cooker if necessary; see the manufacturer's handbook. Heat the oil in a skillet, add the lamb a few pieces at a time until all the pieces are added to the pan, then fry over a high heat, stirring until browned. Remove from the pan with a slotted spoon and transfer to the slow cooker pot.

Add the onion to the skillet and fry, stirring, for 5 minutes or until softened and just beginning to turn golden. Stir in the garlic and ginger, then mix in the flour. Gradually stir in the stock. Add the spices, figs, and a little salt and pepper and bring to a boil, stirring.

Spoon into the slow cooker pot, cover with the lid, and cook on low for 8–10 hours or until the lamb is tender. Stir, then sprinkle with toasted slivered almonds. Serve with lemon and chickpea couscous.

To make couscous, put 1 cup couscous in a bowl with the grated zest and juice of 1 lemon, 2 tablespoons olive oil, 13½ oz can drained chickpeas, 1¾ cups boiling water, and season with salt and pepper. Stand for 5 minutes then fork in 4 tablespoons chopped cilantro.

PREPARATION TIME **15 minutes**

COOKING TEMPERATURE **low**

COOKING TIME **9–10 hours**

SERVES **4**

$\mathcal{B}$eery barley beef

1 tablespoon sunflower oil

1¼ lb lean stewing beef, cubed

1 onion, chopped

1 tablespoon all-purpose flour

8 oz carrots, diced

8 oz parsnips or potatoes, diced

1¼ cups English beer

3 cups beef stock

small bunch of mixed herbs or dried
    bouquet garni

½ cup pearl barley

salt and pepper

Preheat the slow cooker if necessary; see the manufacturer's handbook. Heat the oil in a skillet, add the beef a few pieces at a time until it is all in the pan, then fry over a high heat, stirring, until browned. Remove the beef with a slotted spoon and transfer to the slow cooker pot.

Add the onion to the skillet and fry, stirring, for 5 minutes or until lightly browned. Mix in the flour, then add the diced vegetables and beer and bring to a boil, stirring. Pour into the slow cooker pot.

Add the stock to the skillet with the herbs and a little salt and pepper, bring to a boil, then pour into the slow cooker pot. Stir in the pearl barley, cover with the lid, and cook on low for 9–10 hours until the beef is tender.

Pearl barley swells as it cooks so you may find that you need to add a little extra stock at the end of the cooking time or when you are reheating any leftovers to avoid the dish drying out.

PREPARATION TIME **20 minutes**

COOKING TEMPERATURE **low**

COOKING TIME **6$\frac{1}{4}$–8$\frac{1}{4}$ hours**

SERVES **4**

$\mathscr{S}$weet & sour chicken

1 tablespoon sunflower oil

8 small chicken thighs, about 2 lb in total, skinned, boned, and cubed

4 scallions, thickly sliced; white and green parts kept separate

2 carrots, halved lengthwise and thinly sliced

1 inch fresh ginger root, peeled and finely chopped

14$\frac{1}{4}$ oz can pineapple chunks in natural juice

1$\frac{1}{4}$ cups chicken stock

1 tablespoon cornstarch

1 tablespoon tomato paste

2 tablespoons superfine sugar

2 tablespoons soy sauce

2 tablespoons malt vinegar

7$\frac{1}{2}$ oz can bamboo shoots, drained

1 cup bean sprouts

4 oz snow peas thinly sliced

rice, to serve

Preheat the slow cooker if necessary; see the manufacturer's handbook. Heat the oil in a skillet, add the chicken thighs and fry, stirring, until browned on all sides. Mix in the white scallion slices, carrots, and ginger and cook for 2 minutes.

Stir in the pineapple chunks with their juice and the stock. Put the cornstarch, tomato paste, and sugar into a small bowl, then gradually mix in the soy sauce and vinegar to make a smooth paste. Stir into the pan and bring to a boil, stirring.

Tip the chicken and sauce into the slow cooker pot, add the bamboo shoots, and press the chicken beneath the surface of the sauce. Cover with the lid and cook on low for 6–8 hours.

When almost ready to serve, add the green scallion slices, the bean sprouts, and snow peas to the slow cooker pot and mix well. Replace the lid and cook, still on low, for 15 minutes or until the vegetables are just tender. Serve spooned into rice-filled bowls.

Chilied beef

with cheesy tortillas

1 tablespoon sunflower oil

1 lb extra lean ground beef

1 onion, chopped

2 garlic cloves, finely chopped

1 teaspoon smoked paprika (pimenton)

$^{1}/_{2}$ teaspoon crushed red pepper

1 teaspoon ground cumin

1 tablespoon all-purpose flour

13 oz can chopped tomatoes

13$^{1}/_{2}$ oz can red kidney beans, drained

$^{2}/_{3}$ cup beef stock

1 tablespoon dark brown sugar

salt and pepper

TOPPING

4 oz tortilla chips

$^{1}/_{2}$ red bell pepper, cored, seeded, and diced

chopped cilantro leaves

1 cup grated aged cheddar cheese

Preheat the slow cooker if necessary; see the manufacturer's handbook. Heat the oil in a skillet, add the beef and onion and fry, stirring, for 5 minutes, breaking up the meat with a spoon until it is browned.

Stir in the garlic, paprika, crushed red pepper, and cumin and cook for 2 minutes. Stir in the flour. Mix in the tomatoes, kidney beans, stock, and sugar, season with salt and pepper, and pour the mixture into the slow cooker pot. Cover with the lid and cook on low for 8–10 hours.

Stir the mixture, then arrange the tortilla chips on top. Sprinkle with the bell pepper, cilantro, and cheddar, lift the pot out of the housing using oven mitts and brown under a preheated hot broiler until the cheese just melts. Spoon into bowls to serve.

If you have any beef left over from this dish, serve it spooned over baked potatoes or sweet potatoes then top with sour cream and grated cheddar cheese and sprinkle with a handful of torn cilantro leaves.

$\mathcal{M}$ackerel kedgeree

1 tablespoon sunflower oil

1 onion, chopped

1 teaspoon turmeric

2 tablespoons mango chutney

3–3¾ cups vegetable stock

1 bay leaf

¾ cup easy-cook brown rice

8 oz or 3 smoked mackerel fillets, skinned

⅔ cup frozen peas

½ cup watercress or arugula leaves

salt and pepper

4 hard-cooked eggs, cut into wedges, to garnish

Preheat the slow cooker if necessary; see the manufacturer's handbook. Heat the oil in a skillet, add the onion and fry, stirring, for 5 minutes or until softened and just beginning to turn golden.

Stir in the turmeric, chutney, stock, bay leaf, and a little salt and pepper and bring to a boil. Pour into the slow cooker pot and add the rice. Add the smoked mackerel to the pot in a single layer. Cover with the lid and cook on low for 3–4 hours or until the rice is tender and has absorbed almost all the stock.

Stir in the peas, breaking up the fish into chunky pieces. Add extra hot stock if needed. Cook for 15 minutes more. Stir in the watercress or arugula, spoon onto plates, and serve garnished with wedges of egg.

Spiced meatballs
with dill sauce

1 onion, quartered

2 oz bread

8 oz ground pork

8 oz ground beef

1 teaspoon ground mixed spice

1 egg yolk

1 tablespoon sunflower oil

salt and pepper

SAUCE

1 tablespoon butter

1 onion, sliced

2 tablespoons all-purpose flour

2½ cups chicken stock

4 teaspoons chopped dill weed,
    plus extra to garnish

Preheat the slow cooker if necessary; see the manufacturer's handbook. Finely chop the onion and bread in a food processor or blender. Add the ground meats, mixed spice, egg yolk, and a little salt and pepper and mix together.

Divide the meat mixture into 24 pieces and roll into balls with wetted hands. Heat the oil in a skillet, add the meatballs, and fry over a medium heat, turning until evenly browned but not cooked through. Drain and transfer to the slow cooker pot.

Make the sauce. Add the butter and onion to a clean skillet. Fry, stirring, for 5 minutes or until the onion is softened and just beginning to turn golden. Stir in the flour, then gradually mix in the stock and bring to a boil, stirring. Season with salt and pepper and pour the sauce over the meatballs. Cover with the lid and cook on low for 6–8 hours.

Stir the chopped dill into the sauce and serve the meatballs with mashed potato sprinkled with a little extra chopped dill to garnish.

Short-cut suppers

The beauty of slow cooking is that you can get supper on the go before leaving for work or a trip out. If you have to make an early start in the morning you can part-prepare the recipes in this chapter the night before, then put the ingredients into the slow cooker with hot liquid.

$\mathcal{B}$arley risotto
with blue cheese butter

¾ cup pearl barley

1 onion, finely chopped

2 garlic cloves, finely chopped

1 lb butternut squash, peeled, seeded, and cut into ¾ inch pieces

4 cups boiling vegetable stock

2½ cups baby spinach, washed and well drained

BLUE CHEESE BUTTER

½ cup butter at room temperature

4 oz blue cheese, rind removed

1 garlic clove, finely chopped

¼ teaspoon crushed red pepper

salt and pepper

Preheat the slow cooker if necessary; see the manufacturer's handbook. Put the pearl barley, onion, garlic, and butternut squash in the slow cooker pot. Add the stock and a little salt and pepper. Cover with the lid and cook on low for 6–8 hours or until the barley and squash are tender.

Meanwhile, make the blue cheese butter. Put the butter on a plate, crumble the cheese on top, add the garlic and crushed pepper and mash together with a fork. Spoon the butter into a line on a piece of nonstick parchment paper, then wrap it in paper and roll it backward and forward to make a neat sausage shape. Chill until required.

When almost ready to serve, stir the risotto, slice half the butter and add to the slow cooker pot. Mix together until just beginning to melt, then add the spinach. Replace the lid and cook, still on low, for 15 minutes until the spinach has just wilted. Ladle into shallow bowls and serve topped with slices of the remaining butter.

To save time in the morning, put the barley, vegetables, and garlic in a plastic-wrapped bowl in the refrigerator and prepare the butter the night before. The next day, crumble a stock cube into a measuring cup of boiling water and add everything to the slow cooker.

PREPARATION TIME **20 minutes**

COOKING TEMPERATURE **high and low**

COOKING TIME **8–10 hours**

SERVES **4**

Chicken & mascarpone
pasta bake

1 lb boneless, skinless chicken thighs, cut into chunks

1 onion, finely chopped

1 red and 1 orange bell pepper, cored, seeded, and diced

6 sun-dried tomatoes in oil, drained and sliced

2 garlic cloves, finely chopped

1 tablespoon cornstarch

13 oz can chopped tomatoes

1 chicken bouillon cube

1 cup water

10 oz penne

3 oz mascarpone cheese

small bunch of basil

salt and pepper

Preheat the slow cooker if necessary; see the manufacturer's handbook. Put the chicken, onion, peppers, sun-dried tomatoes, and garlic into the slow cooker. Mix the cornstarch in a small bowl with a little water to make a smooth paste and add this to the slow cooker.

Pour the tomatoes into a microproof measuring cup, crumble in the bouillon cube, add the water, and cook on full power for $2^{1}/_{2}$ minutes until piping hot. Season with salt and pepper and pour into the slow cooker pot.

Mix together, then cover with the lid and cook on high for 30 minutes. Reduce to low and cook for $7^{1}/_{2}$–$9^{1}/_{2}$ hours or set to auto for 8–10 hours.

When almost ready to serve, add the pasta to a saucepan of boiling water and cook for 8–10 minutes until just tender. Stir the mascarpone cheese into the chicken with half the basil leaves.

Drain the pasta and stir into the sauce. Spoon into shallow bowls and serve sprinkled with the remaining basil leaves.

Mascarpone cheese adds a wonderful creaminess to this garlicky tomato sauce, but you could stir in a garlic and herb full-fat cream cheese or a few tablespoons of cream if you don't have any mascarpone.

Smoked cod
with cannellini bean mash

2 x 13½ oz cans cannellini beans, drained

1 bunch of scallions, thinly sliced; white and green parts kept separate

1¾ cups boiling fish stock

1 teaspoon grainy mustard

grated zest and juice of 1 lemon

4 smoked cod loins, about 1¼ lb in total

4 tablespoons full-fat sour cream

small bunch of parsley, watercress, or arugula leaves, roughly chopped

salt and pepper

Preheat the slow cooker if necessary; see the manufacturer's handbook. Add the drained beans to the slow cooker with the white scallion slices. Mix the fish stock with the mustard, lemon zest and juice, and a little salt and pepper, then pour into the slow cooker pot.

Arrange the fish on top and sprinkle with a little extra pepper. Cover with the lid and cook on low for 1½–2 hours or until the fish flakes easily when pressed in the center with a knife.

Remove the fish with a slotted spoon and transfer to a plate. Pour off nearly all the cooking liquid, then mash the beans roughly. Stir in the sour cream, the remaining scallion, and the parsley, watercress, or arugula. Taste and add salt and pepper if needed. Spoon the mash on to plates and top with the fish.

Most of us don't have time to make homemade stock, so make up a low-salt bouillon cube with boiling water, making sure it has completely dissolved, then add the liquid directly to the slow cooker pot.

PREPARATION TIME **25 minutes, plus marinating**

COOKING TEMPERATURE **high and low**

COOKING TIME **10–11 hours**

SERVES **4**

tifado

¾ **cup red wine**

1 tablespoon tomato paste

2 tablespoons olive oil

2–3 stems of thyme or bay leaves

4 cloves

¼ **teaspoon ground allspice**

10 oz shallots, halved if large

2 garlic cloves, finely chopped

1½ **lb stewing beef, cut into large chunks and any fat discarded**

4 teaspoons cornstarch

⅔ **cup cold water**

½ **bouillon cube**

salt and pepper

TO SERVE

toasted, sliced French bread

herb butter

The night before, mix the wine, tomato paste, and oil in a shallow, nonmetallic dish. Add the herbs, spices, and some salt and pepper and mix together. Then add the shallots and garlic. Add the beef, toss in the marinade, cover with plastic wrap, and chill overnight in the refrigerator.

Preheat the slow cooker if necessary; see the manufacturer's handbook. Put the cornstarch in a saucepan, mix in a little of the water to make a smooth paste, then mix in the remaining water. Drain the marinade from the beef into the pan and crumble in the bouillon cube. Bring to a boil, stirring.

Tip the beef, shallots, and flavorings into the slow cooker pot, pour over the hot stock mixture, cover with the lid, and cook on high for 30 minutes. Reduce to low and cook for 9½–10½ hours or set to auto for 10–11 hours until the meat is tender.

Spoon into bowls and serve with toasted French bread spread with a herb butter.

This aromatic Greek stew was traditionally cooked overnight in an outdoor clay oven, making it an ideal recipe to adapt for the slow cooker. The marinade may also be used for rabbit or chicken portions.

PREPARATION TIME **20 minutes**

COOKING TEMPERATURE **high and low**

COOKING TIME **8–10 hours**

SERVES **4**

$\mathcal{M}$oroccan lamb

1 onion, thinly sliced

2 carrots, diced

8 oz rutabaga, diced

1½ inches fresh ginger root, peeled and finely chopped

grated zest of 1 lemon

2 teaspoons harissa (Moroccan chili paste)

½ teaspoon ground allspice

1 lb 6 oz lamb leg steaks

1 tablespoon cornstarch

13 oz can chopped tomatoes

⅔ cup lamb stock

salt and pepper

lemon wedges, to garnish

TO SERVE

couscous

pita bread

Preheat the slow cooker if necessary; see the manufacturer's handbook. Put the onion and diced vegetables into the slow cooker pot, add the ginger, lemon zest, harissa, and allspice and arrange the lamb steaks on top.

Mix the cornstarch to a smooth paste with a little water in a small bowl. Put the tomatoes and stock in a saucepan, mix in the cornstarch paste and some salt and pepper and bring to a boil; alternatively, heat in a microwave if you prefer. Pour over the lamb.

Cover with the lid and cook on high for 30 minutes. Reduce to low and cook for 7½–9½ hours or set to auto for 8–10 hours or until the lamb is tender. Garnish with lemon wedges and serve with couscous tossed with the juice of 1 lemon and toasted pita bread.

The vegetables, ginger, and lemon zest can be prepared the night before and put into a plastic bag in the refrigerator. If you really like garlic, add 2 finely chopped garlic cloves or add some ready-prepared garlic puree from a jar.

$\mathcal{T}$omato braised squid
with chorizo

1¼ lb chilled squid

1 onion, thinly sliced

4 oz ready-diced chorizo

4 oz button mushrooms, sliced

1 red bell pepper, cored, seeded, and sliced

2 garlic cloves, finely chopped

2–3 sprigs of rosemary, leaves stripped from the stems

1 tablespoon tomato paste

1 teaspoon superfine sugar

13 oz can chopped tomatoes

6 tablespoons red wine

1 tablespoon cornstarch

salt and pepper

chopped parsley, to garnish

rice or thickly sliced bread, to serve

Preheat the slow cooker if necessary; see the manufacturer's handbook. Rinse the squid inside and out, pulling out the tentacles and reserving. Drain and slice the bodies. Put the tentacles in a bowl, cover with plastic wrap, and refrigerate.

Put the onion, chorizo, mushrooms, and red pepper in the slow cooker pot. Add the garlic, rosemary, tomato paste, and sugar, then stir in the sliced squid.

Pour the tomatoes and wine into a saucepan and bring to a boil; alternatively, heat in a microwave if you prefer. Add a little salt and pepper, then pour the mixture into the slow cooker pot and stir all ingredients together.

Cover with the lid and cook on low for 3–5 hours or until the squid is tender.

When almost ready to serve, mix the cornstarch to a paste with a little water in a small bowl. Stir into the slow cooker pot, add the squid tentacles, then replace the lid and cook on low for 30 minutes. Spoon the squid mixture into bowls lined with rice and serve sprinkled with chopped parsley, or serve with thickly sliced bread instead.

The secret of succulent squid is to cook it either very fast in a skillet or very slowly, as here, with wine and tomatoes. The chorizo adds a depth and spiciness to the sauce.

PREPARATION TIME **30 minutes**

COOKING TEMPERATURE **high and low**

COOKING TIME **6–8 hours**

SERVES **4**

*C*hicken avgolemono

8 boneless, skinless chicken thighs, about 1 lb 6 oz in total

1 onion, thinly sliced

2–3 stems of oregano or basil

1¾ cups boiling chicken stock

grated zest and juice of 1 lemon

10 oz macaroni or orzo pasta

2 whole eggs

2 egg yolks

4 tablespoons chopped parsley, plus extra to garnish (optional)

salt and pepper

lemon rind curls, to garnish (optional)

Preheat the slow cooker if necessary; see the manufacturer's handbook. Put the chicken, onion, and oregano or basil into the slow cooker pot. Mix the stock with the lemon zest and juice and some salt and pepper. Pour the liquid over the chicken.

Cover with the lid and cook on high for 30 minutes. Reduce to low and cook for 5½–6½ hours or set to auto for 6–8 hours or until the chicken is tender.

When almost ready to serve, bring a large saucepan of water to a boil, add the pasta, and cook for 9–10 minutes until just tender.

Meanwhile, drain the stock from the slow cooker into a second large saucepan and boil for 5 minutes until reduced by one-third or to about ¾ cup.

Beat the eggs and egg yolks in a bowl, then gradually beat in 2 ladlefuls of stock until smooth. Pour into the saucepan with the remaining stock, then beat over a gentle heat until the sauce has thickened slightly. Stir in the parsley and check the seasoning.

Pour the sauce over the chicken. Spoon the pasta into shallow serving bowls and top with the chicken. Garnish with lemon rind curls and extra chopped parsley, if desired.

This simple sauce is easy to make, but it will need some careful watching while the eggs are cooking, as if it boils it will curdle in the same way as a sweet custard sauce.

$\mathcal{H}$am in cola

2½ lb boneless smoked ham joint, soaked overnight in cold water

5 cloves

1 onion, cut into 8 wedges

2 carrots, thickly sliced

13½ oz can black beans or red kidney beans, drained

2 bay leaves

3¾ cups cola

1 tablespoon dark brown sugar

1 tablespoon tomato paste

2 teaspoons English mustard

Preheat the slow cooker if necessary; see the manufacturer's handbook. Drain the ham joint and put it into the slow cooker pot. Press the cloves into 5 of the onion wedges and add to the ham with the remaining onion wedges and carrot slices. Tip in the drained beans and add the bay leaves.

Pour the cola into a saucepan, add the sugar, tomato paste, and mustard and bring to a boil, stirring. Pour over the ham, cover with the lid, and cook on high for 6–7 hours or until the ham is tender.

Strain the cooking liquid into a saucepan and boil rapidly for 10 minutes to reduce by half. Keep the ham and vegetables hot in the turned-off slow cooker with the lid on.

Slice the ham thinly and arrange on plates with the vegetables, beans, and a drizzle of sauce.

PREPARATION TIME **5 minutes**

COOKING TEMPERATURE **high and low**

COOKING TIME **8–10 hours**

SERVES **4**

$\mathcal{B}$oston baked beans

1 onion, finely chopped

2 carrots, diced

13½ oz can black eye beans, drained

13½ oz can cranberry beans, drained

2 bay leaves

2 teaspoons English mustard

1 tablespoon cornstarch

1 tablespoon molasses

2 tablespoons tomato paste

2 tablespoons light brown sugar

2 tablespoons malt or red wine vinegar

1 chicken bouillon cube

1¾ cups boiling water

1½ lb rindless pork belly slices

salt and pepper

garlic or herb bread, to serve (optional)

Preheat the slow cooker if necessary; see the manufacturer's handbook. Add the onion, carrots, drained beans, and bay leaves to the slow cooker pot and mix together.

In a bowl mix together the mustard, cornstarch, molasses, tomato paste, sugar, and vinegar. Crumble in the bouillon cube, then gradually mix in the boiling water. Tip into the slow cooker and stir together.

Add the belly pork slices in a single layer and press beneath the level of the liquid. Cover with the lid and cook on high for 30 minutes. Reduce to low and cook for 7½–9½ hours or set to auto for 8–10 hours. Serve with hot garlic or herb bread, if desired.

Canned beans have been used here to save time, but you can also use dried ones. Soak them overnight in plenty of cold water, then bring to a boil in a pan of fresh water. Boil rapidly for 10 minutes, then drain and add to the slow cooker pot.

PREPARATION TIME **15 minutes**

COOKING TEMPERATURE **high**

COOKING TIME **1¹/₂–2 hours**

SERVES **4**

$\mathcal{H}$ot soused herring

1 large red onion, thinly sliced

1 large carrot, cut into matchsticks

1 large celery stick, thinly sliced

6 small herrings, gutted, filleted, and
    rinsed with cold water

2 stems of tarragon, plus extra sprigs
    to garnish

1 bay leaf

²/₃ cup cider vinegar

2 tablespoons superfine sugar

2¹/₂ cups boiling water

¹/₂ teaspoon mixed peppercorns

salt

Preheat the slow cooker if necessary; see the manufacturer's
handbook. Put half the onion, carrot, and celery in the slow cooker
pot. Arrange the herring fillets on top, then cover them with the
remaining vegetables.

Add the tarragon, bay leaf, vinegar, and sugar. Pour over the boiling
water and add the peppercorns and a little salt. Cover with the lid and
cook on high for 1¹/₂–2 hours or until the fish flakes when pressed with
a knife.

Spoon the fish, vegetables, and a little of the cooking liquid into
shallow bowls, halving the fish fillets, if desired. Garnish with tarragon
sprigs. Serve with pickled beet, dill cucumbers, and bread and butter,
if desired.

PREPARATION TIME **20 minutes**

COOKING TEMPERATURE **high and low**

COOKING TIME **8–10 hours**

SERVES **4**

$\mathcal{P}$ork goulash

1 onion, finely chopped

2 cups finely shredded red cabbage

1 teaspoon caraway seeds

1 teaspoon paprika

¼ teaspoon ground allspice

½ teaspoon crushed red pepper

4 teaspoons cornstarch

1 tablespoon light brown sugar

2 tablespoons tomato paste

2 tablespoons red wine vinegar

4 pork loin chops, about 2 lb in total

1¾ cups boiling chicken stock

salt and pepper

garlic bread, to serve (optional)

TO GARNISH

sour cream

paprika

crushed red pepper

Preheat the slow cooker if necessary; see the manufacturer's handbook. Put the onion and red cabbage into the slow cooker pot. Mix the seeds, spices, and crushed pepper in a small bowl with the cornstarch, sugar, tomato paste, and vinegar. Put the pork chops on top of the cabbage and pour the spice mix on top.

Pour over the stock, add a little salt and pepper, then cover and cook on high for 30 minutes. Reduce to low and cook for 7½–9½ hours or set to auto for 8–10 hours or until the pork and cabbage are tender.

Spoon the goulash into shallow bowls, top with spoonfuls of sour cream and a sprinkling of paprika and extra crushed pepper. Serve with garlic bread, if desired.

Forgotten cuts

The old-fashioned cuts our grandmothers used to cook are making a trendy comeback. They're cheap and readily available, and they taste better the longer they cook, making them perfect for your slow cooker.

$\mathcal{P}$ot-roast beef
with brown ale

2 lb beef brisket

2–3 stems of rosemary

8 slices bacon

2 tablespoons butter

2 tablespoons all-purpose flour

1¼ cups English beer

1¼ cups beef stock

2 teaspoons grainy mustard

1 tablespoon tomato paste

4 baby parsnips, quartered

8 oz chantenay carrots, any large
ones halved

1 leek, thickly sliced

salt and pepper

crusty bread, to serve (optional)

Preheat the slow cooker if necessary; see the manufacturer's handbook. Remove the string from the beef, tuck the rosemary into the center, then wrap the sides with the bacon and tie in place with fresh string.

Heat the butter in a skillet, add the beef, and fry the bacon-wrapped edges until they are browned. Transfer the beef to the slow cooker pot. Stir the flour into the pan juices, then mix in the beer, stock, mustard, and tomato paste. Add a little salt and pepper and bring to a boil, stirring.

Pour the mixture over the beef, add the vegetables and press beneath the surface of the liquid. Cover and cook on high for 5–6 hours or until the vegetables are tender.

Lift the beef onto a cutting board and cut it into thin slices, discarding the string and rosemary stems. Arrange in shallow serving bowls and add the vegetables and a ladleful of beery juices to each one. Serve with warm crusty bread for dunking, if desired.

Brisket has a coarser texture than more traditional roasting joints, so carve it into thin slices and serve with lots of the cooking juices. Any leftover cooking juices make a great base for a soup with extra vegetables or a mix of vegetables and lentils.

Stuffed breast of lamb

1 breast of lamb, about 1½ lb

13 oz specialty flavored sausages such as Toulouse or Sicilian

½ cup ready-to-eat dried apricots, chopped

1 tablespoon olive oil

1 onion, sliced

2 tablespoons all-purpose flour

1¾ cups lamb stock

2–3 stems of rosemary

1 tablespoon tomato paste

salt and pepper

TO SERVE

rice

green beans

Preheat the slow cooker if necessary; see the manufacturer's handbook. Remove the string from the breast of lamb and open it out flat on a cutting board. Cut along the length of each sausage and peel off the skin. Press the sausagemeat over the lamb and sprinkle with the chopped apricots. Roll up the lamb and tie at intervals with string.

Heat the oil in a skillet, add the lamb and brown on all sides, adding the onions halfway through and frying these until softened.

Transfer the lamb to the slow cooker pot. Stir the flour into the onion, then mix in the stock, rosemary, tomato paste, and a little salt and pepper. Bring to a boil and pour over the lamb.

Cover with the lid and cook on high for 6–7 hours or until the lamb is very tender. Cut into 8 slices, discarding the string, and serve in shallow bowls on a bed of rice with green beans, spooning the cooking juices around.

This is an excellent budget-friendly roast. Breast of lamb is extremely cheap and mixed with gourmet flavored sausages it easily serves four hungry people. It is also delicious served on a bed of mashed mixed roots or mashed sweet potato with chopped chili.

Turkey tagine

1 turkey drumstick, about 1 lb 6 oz

1 tablespoon olive oil

1 onion, chopped

2 garlic cloves, finely chopped

1 inch fresh ginger root, peeled and finely chopped

2 tablespoons all-purpose flour

1 teaspoon turmeric

1 teaspoon ground cinnamon

1 teaspoon ground coriander

$\frac{1}{2}$ teaspoon cumin seeds

$2\frac{1}{2}$ cups boiling chicken stock

$13\frac{1}{2}$ oz can chickpeas, drained

$1\frac{1}{2}$ cups diced parsnips

$1\frac{1}{2}$ cups diced carrots

salt and pepper

small bunch of cilantro, roughly chopped

TO SERVE

rice or couscous

naan bread

Check that the turkey drumstick will fit into the slow cooker pot before you begin, cutting off the knuckle end if needed with a large knife and hitting it with a rolling pin or hammer to sever. Preheat the slow cooker if necessary; see the manufacturer's handbook.

Heat the oil in a skillet, add the drumstick and fry, turning, until golden-brown all over. Transfer to the slow cooker pot. Add the onion to the pan and fry until softened. Stir in the garlic, ginger, and flour, then mix in the spices. Gradually stir in the stock, season to taste with salt and pepper and bring to a boil.

Pour the onion mixture over the turkey. Add the chickpeas and vegetables to the pot and press beneath the stock. Cover with the lid and cook on high for 6–7 hours or until the meat is tender and almost falling off the bone.

Lift the turkey drumstick out of the slow cooker pot and take the meat off the bone, discarding the skin and tendons. Cut it into bite-size pieces and return them to the slow cooker pot. Stir in the chopped cilantro and serve with rice or couscous and naan bread.

Turkey drumsticks are a good-value cut and needn't be thought of as something to eat only at Thanksgiving or Christmas time. Sold all the year round in supermarkets, they really suit long, slow cooking and can be mixed with Moroccan or Indian spice blends.

Oxtail bredie

1–2 tablespoons sunflower oil

2 lb oxtail

2 onions, sliced

1 inch fresh ginger root, peeled and finely chopped

1/2 teaspoon crushed red pepper

1/2 teaspoon ground cinnamon

1 teaspoon ground cumin

2 tablespoons all-purpose flour

13 oz can chopped tomatoes

1 1/4 cups beef stock

2 bay leaves

2 tablespoons light brown sugar

2 tablespoons malt vinegar

salt and pepper

chopped parsley or cilantro, to garnish

mashed sweet potatoes, to serve

Preheat the slow cooker if necessary; see the manufacturer's handbook. Heat 1 tablespoon of the oil in a skillet, add the oxtail, and fry until browned on all sides. Lift it out of the pan with a slotted spoon and put it into the slow cooker pot.

Add the onion to the pan with a little extra oil and fry for 5 minutes until softened and lightly browned. Stir in the ginger, red pepper, and ground spices, then add the flour. Gradually mix in the tomatoes and stock. Stir in the bay leaves, sugar, vinegar, and a little salt and pepper.

Bring the mixture to a boil, spoon into the slow cooker pot, cover, and cook on low for 9–10 hours or until the oxtail is tender and almost falling off the bones. Serve scooped onto mashed sweet potatoes and sprinkled with a little chopped parsley or cilantro.

There are many versions of this tomato-based bredie, the Afrikaans name for a South African tomato stew. They are mostly made with mutton, but the cinnamon, chili, and sweet, slightly sour sauce also complement the richness of oxtail.

PREPARATION TIME **20 minutes**

COOKING TEMPERATURE **low**

COOKING TIME **6–7 hours**

SERVES **4**

Normandy rabbit

2 tablespoons all-purpose flour

1 rabbit, cut into 4 pieces

1 tablespoon olive oil

2 tablespoons butter

1 large onion, sliced

2 sharp dessert apples, such as Granny Smith, cored and quartered

3 tablespoons Calvados or brandy

1 cup chicken stock

$^2/_3$ cup Normandy cider

3 teaspoons grainy mustard

4 tablespoons sour cream (optional)

salt and pepper

TO SERVE

sugar snap peas

baby new potatoes

parsley

Preheat the slow cooker if necessary; see the manufacturer's handbook. Put the flour on a plate, mix with a little salt and pepper, and use it to dust the rabbit pieces all over.

Heat the oil and butter in a skillet, add the rabbit pieces, and brown on both sides. Lift out and transfer to the slow cooker pot.

Add the onion to the pan and fry, stirring, until lightly browned. Add the apples and Calvados or brandy and bring to a boil. Light the brandy with a long taper and stand well back until the flames subside.

Mix in the stock, cider, mustard, and a little salt and pepper. Bring to a boil, then pour over the rabbit. Cover with the lid and cook on low for 6–7 hours. Stir the sauce. Mix in the sour cream (if used) and serve with sugar snap peas and roughly crushed baby new potatoes mixed with a little chopped parsley.

Rabbit goes well with cider and brandy in this Normandy version of *coq au vin.* **You can use chicken thigh and leg joints instead, or try the recipe with 8 large pork sausages, but omit the flaming Calvados or brandy stage and serve without the sour cream.**

Alsace-style pork

1 tablespoon sunflower oil

1 onion, chopped

1 dessert apple, cored and diced

4 tomatoes, diced

1 teaspoon caraway seeds

1¼ cups blond beer

⅔ cup chicken stock

1½ cups sauerkraut, drained

2 lb large pork hock

4 dried pork kabanos sausages, about
4 oz, halved

2 carrots, diced

2–3 pickled dill cucumbers, about
4 oz sliced

salt and pepper

chopped parsley, to garnish

rye bread, to serve (optional)

Preheat the slow cooker if necessary; see the manufacturer's handbook. Heat the oil in a skillet, add the onion, and fry, stirring, for 5 minutes or until softened. Add the apple, tomatoes, caraway seeds, beer, and stock. Season with salt and pepper and bring to a boil.

Tip into the slow cooker pot, add the drained sauerkraut and stir together. Press the pork hock into the center, then add the sausages, carrots, and dill cucumbers and press into the liquid. Cover with the lid and cook on high for 6–7 hours.

Sprinkle the hock with chopped parsley and serve straight from the pot or lift it out of the slow cooker, take off the skin, and remove the bone. Cut the meat into bite-size pieces and spoon back into the slow cooker. Sprinkle with parsley and serve in shallow bowls topped with the sauce and accompanied with rye bread, if desired.

Cut from the arm shoulder, a pork hock is the lower part of the foreleg, and you will need to ask the butcher to cut it for you. Any leftover gravy will set to a jelly when it is cold.

*H*am hock with lentils
& chilied squash

2–2¹/₂ lb smoked bacon hock, soaked overnight in cold water

1 cup Puy lentils

2 small onions, cut into thick wedges

1 small butternut squash, cut into 4–6 slices and seeds scooped out (leave the skin on)

2 bay leaves

1 teaspoon fennel seeds

¹/₂–³/₄ teaspoon crushed red pepper

3 cups boiling water

pepper

small bunch of parsley, roughly chopped, to garnish (optional)

Preheat the slow cooker if necessary; see the manufacturer's handbook. Drain the bacon joint and put it in the slow cooker pot. Add the lentils, onions, and squash. Add the bay leaves, sprinkle with the fennel seeds, red pepper, and a little pepper, then pour in the boiling water.

Cover with the lid and cook on high for 6–7 hours or until the bacon is tender and the lentils are soft.

Lift the bacon out of the slow cooker pot and put it on a serving dish. Peel away the rind and remove the bone, then cut the meat into chunks. Spoon the lentils and vegetables into shallow bowls, then top with the meat. Sprinkle with the parsley, if desired, and serve the remaining cooking juices ladled into a pitcher or bowl for diners to add as required.

Leaving the squash skin in place during cooking stops the flesh from falling apart, but if you can't get a small butternut squash, cut 1 lb from a larger one and cut it into 4 pieces. Bacon hocks can be salty so add salt to taste at the very end.

PREPARATION TIME **15 minutes**

COOKING TEMPERATURE **high**

COOKING TIME **6–7 hours**

SERVES **4**

$\mathcal{N}$avarin of lamb
with spring vegetables

1 tablespoon olive oil

2 lb neck of lamb or a supermarket package of mixed stewing lamb pieces

13 oz baby new potatoes, scrubbed and halved if large

8 oz shallots, halved if large

2 garlic cloves, finely chopped (optional)

2 tablespoons all-purpose flour

2½ cups lamb stock

2 teaspoons tomato paste

1 teaspoon Dijon mustard

1 fresh or dried bouquet garni

salt and pepper

TO FINISH

¾ cup green beans, halved

4 oz thin asparagus spears, stems halved

½ cup frozen fava beans or peas

3 tablespoons chopped parsley (optional)

Preheat the slow cooker if necessary; see the manufacturer's handbook. Heat the oil in a skillet, add the lamb pieces, and fry until browned on both sides. Lift out of the pan with a slotted spoon and add to the slow cooker pot with the potatoes.

Add the shallots and garlic (if used) to the skillet, fry until lightly browned, then stir in the flour. Gradually mix in the stock. Add the tomato paste, mustard, bouquet garni, and a little salt and pepper. Bring to a boil, then pour over the lamb.

Cover with the lid and cook on high for 6–7 hours until the lamb is tender. Just before serving put the green vegetables in a small saucepan of boiling water. Simmer for 5 minutes, then drain and toss with the parsley (if used). Stir the lamb and spoon the vegetables on top. Serve in shallow bowls.

Neck of lamb is incredibly cheap, and when it's cooked for a long time it practically falls off the bone. You might prefer to take the meat off the bones before serving, especially if you have young children, or you could use 4 small lamb shanks instead.

Vegetarian

You can do a lot more in your slow cooker than just making meaty casseroles. Try these vegetarian main meals and accompaniments flavored with spices from around the world. And remember: you don't have to make them just for your vegetarian friends.

$\mathcal{M}$ushroom cobbler

2 tablespoons olive oil

1 onion, chopped

2 garlic cloves, chopped

8 oz flat mushrooms, peeled and quartered

8 oz chestnut mushrooms, quartered

1 tablespoon all-purpose flour

¾ cup red wine

13 oz can chopped tomatoes

⅔ cup vegetable stock

1 tablespoon red currant jelly

2–3 stems of thyme

salt and pepper

WALNUT CRUST

1¾ cups self-rising flour

¼ cup butter, diced

⅓ cup chopped walnut pieces

¾ cup grated cheddar cheese

1 egg, beaten

4–5 tablespoons milk

Preheat the slow cooker if necessary; see the manufacturer's handbook. Heat the oil in a skillet, add the onion, garlic, and mushrooms and fry, stirring, for 5 minutes or until just turning golden.

Stir in the flour, then mix in the wine, tomatoes, and stock. Add the red currant jelly, thyme, and salt and pepper and bring to a boil. Pour into the slow cooker pot, cover with the lid, and cook on low for 6–8 hours.

When almost ready to serve, make the topping. Put the flour and butter in a bowl, blend in the butter with your fingertips until the mixture resembles fine bread crumbs. Stir in the walnuts, cheddar, and salt and pepper. Add half the egg, then mix in enough milk to make a soft dough.

Knead lightly, then roll out the dough on a lightly floured surface until ¾ inch thick. Stamp out 8 rounds with a 2½ inch plain cookie cutter, re-rolling the trimmings as needed. Stir the mushroom casserole, then arrange the rounds, slightly overlapping, around the edge of the dish. Cover with the lid and cook on high for 45 minutes or until well risen.

Lift the pot out of the housing using oven mitts, brush the tops of the rounds with the remaining egg and brown under a preheated hot broiler, if desired.

*E*ggplant ratatouille
with ricotta dumplings

3 tablespoons olive oil

1 onion, chopped

1 eggplant, sliced

2 zucchini, about 12 oz in total, sliced

1 red bell pepper, cored, seeded, and diced

1 yellow bell pepper, cored, seeded, and diced

2 garlic cloves, finely chopped

1 tablespoon all-purpose flour

13 oz can chopped tomatoes

1¼ cups vegetable stock

2–3 stems of rosemary

salt and pepper

DUMPLINGS

1 cup all-purpose flour

⅓ cup ricotta cheese

grated zest of ½ lemon

1 egg, beaten

Preheat the slow cooker if necessary; see the manufacturer's handbook. Heat the oil in a skillet, add the onion and eggplant and fry, stirring, for 5 minutes or until softened and beginning to turn golden.

Stir in the zucchini, peppers, and garlic and fry for 3–4 minutes. Mix in the flour, then the tomatoes, stock, rosemary, and a little salt and pepper. Bring to a boil, then spoon into the slow cooker pot. Cover with the lid and cook on high for 3–4 hours until the vegetables are tender.

When almost ready to serve, make the dumplings. Put the flour, ricotta, lemon zest, and a little salt and pepper into a bowl. Add the egg and mix to a soft but not sticky dough. Cut into 12 pieces and roll each piece into a ball with floured hands.

Stir the ratatouille and arrange the dumplings on the top. Replace the lid and cook for 15–20 minutes or until the dumplings are light and firm to the touch.

These lemon-flavored Italian inspired dumplings also taste good added to slow-cooked root vegetable soups or added to more robust mushroom and lentil stews, and even in chilied bean mixtures.

$\mathscr{A}$romatic sweet potato
& egg curry

1 tablespoon sunflower oil

1 onion, chopped

1 teaspoon cumin seeds, roughly crushed

1 teaspoon ground coriander

1 teaspoon turmeric

1 teaspoon garam masala

$^{1}/_{2}$ teaspoon crushed red pepper

2 cups diced sweet potatoes

2 garlic cloves, finely chopped

13 oz can chopped tomatoes

13$^{1}/_{2}$ oz can lentils, drained

1$^{1}/_{4}$ cups vegetable stock

1 teaspoon superfine sugar

6 eggs

1 cup frozen peas

$^{2}/_{3}$ cup heavy cream

small bunch of cilantro, torn into pieces

salt and pepper

rice or naan bread, to serve (optional)

Preheat the slow cooker if necessary; see the manufacturer's handbook. Heat the oil in a skillet, add the onion and fry, stirring, for 5 minutes or until softened and just beginning to turn golden.

Stir in the spices, crushed pepper, sweet potatoes, and garlic and fry for 2 minutes. Add the tomatoes, lentils, stock, and sugar and season with a little salt and pepper. Bring to a boil, stirring. Spoon into the slow cooker pot, cover with the lid, and cook on low for 6–8 hours.

When almost ready to serve, put the eggs in a small saucepan, cover with cold water, bring to a boil, and simmer for 8 minutes. Drain, crack the shells and cool under cold running water. Peel and halve the eggs, then add to the slow cooker pot with the peas, cream, and half the cilantro. Cover with the lid and cook on low for 15 minutes.

Spoon the curry into bowls, garnish with the remaining cilantro, and serve with rice or warm naan bread, if desired.

Zucchini tian

¼ cup long-grain rice

butter, for greasing

1 tomato, sliced

1 tablespoon olive oil

½ onion, chopped

1 garlic clove, finely chopped

1 zucchini, about 6 oz, coarsely
    grated

2½ cups spinach, thickly shredded

3 eggs

6 tablespoons milk

pinch of grated nutmeg

4 tablespoons chopped mint

salt and pepper

Preheat the slow cooker if necessary; see the manufacturer's handbook. Bring a small saucepan of water to a boil, add the rice, bring back to a boil, then simmer for 8–10 minutes or until tender. Meanwhile, butter the inside of a soufflé dish that is 5½ inches in diameter and 3½ inches high. Base-line with nonstick parchment paper, and arrange the tomato slices, overlapping, on the paper.

Heat the oil in a skillet, add the onion and fry, stirring, for 5 minutes or until softened and just beginning to turn golden. Stir in the garlic, then add the zucchini and spinach and cook for 2 minutes or until the spinach is just wilted.

Beat together the eggs, milk, nutmeg, and a little salt and pepper. Drain the rice and stir into the spinach mixture with the egg mixture and mint. Mix well, then spoon into the dish. Cover loosely with buttered foil and lower into the slow cooker pot with foil straps (see page 17) or tie string around the top edge.

Pour boiling water into the slow cooker pot to come halfway up the sides of the dish. Cover with the lid and cook on high for 1½–2 hours or until the tian is set in the middle. Lift out of the slow cooker and allow to stand for 5 minutes.

Remove the foil from the tian, loosen the edge and turn it out onto a plate. Peel off the lining paper, cut into wedges, and serve warm with salad, if desired.

Balsamic tomatoes
with spaghetti

1 tablespoon olive oil

1¹/₂ lb plum tomatoes, halved

4 tablespoons white wine

4 teaspoons good balsamic vinegar

12 oz spaghetti

salt and pepper

TO GARNISH

small bunch of basil

freshly grated or shaved Parmesan
cheese

Preheat the slow cooker if necessary; see the manufacturer's handbook. Brush the oil over the base of the slow cooker pot, add the tomatoes, cut side down, drizzle over the wine and vinegar, and add a little salt and pepper. Cover with the lid and cook on high for 3–4 hours.

When almost ready to serve, bring a large saucepan of water to a boil, add the pasta, and cook for 6–7 minutes or until tender. Drain and mix into the sauce.

Spoon the pasta into bowls and serve sprinkled with basil leaves and grated or shaved Parmesan.

If you prefer a thicker tomato sauce mix a few teaspoons of cornstarch to a paste with some cold water and stir the mixture into the sauce 30 minutes before the end of cooking.

$\mathcal{H}$erby stuffed peppers

4 different colored bell peppers

¹/₂ cup easy-cook brown rice

13¹/₂ oz can chickpeas, drained

small bunch of parsley, roughly chopped

small bunch of mint, roughly chopped

1 onion, finely chopped

2 garlic cloves, finely chopped

¹/₂ teaspoon smoked paprika (pimenton)

1 teaspoon ground allspice

2¹/₂ cups hot vegetable stock

salt and pepper

Preheat the slow cooker if necessary; see the manufacturer's handbook. Cut the top off each pepper and remove the core and seeds.

Mix together the rice, chickpeas, herbs, onion, garlic, paprika, and allspice with plenty of salt and pepper. Spoon the mixture into the peppers, then put the peppers into the slow cooker pot.

Pour the hot stock around the peppers, cover with the lid, and cook on low for 4–5 hours or until the rice and peppers are tender.

Spoon the peppers into dishes and serve with salad and spoonfuls of plain yogurt flavored with extra chopped herbs, if desired.

You can vary the herbs used in this recipe, so why not try using chopped basil and chives or rosemary and parsley instead? If you have one or two tomatoes, dice them and then add to the stuffing, too.

*S*panish baked potatoes

2 tablespoons olive oil

1 large red onion, thinly sliced

2 garlic cloves, finely chopped

1 teaspoon smoked paprika (pimenton)

$^1/_4$–$^1/_2$ teaspoon (or to taste) crushed red pepper

1 red bell pepper, cored, seeded, and diced

1 yellow bell pepper, cored, seeded, and diced

13 oz can chopped tomatoes

1$^1/_4$ cups vegetable stock

2–3 stems of thyme

$^1/_3$ cup pitted dry olives

1$^1/_4$ lb baking potatoes, cut into 1 inch chunks

salt and pepper

crusty bread, to serve

Preheat the slow cooker if necessary; see the manufacturer's handbook. Heat the oil in a skillet, add the onion and fry, stirring, for 5 minutes or until just beginning to turn golden.

Stir in the garlic, paprika, crushed pepper, and peppers and cook for 2 minutes. Mix in the tomatoes, stock, thyme, olives, and some salt and pepper, then bring to a boil.

Add the potatoes to the slow cooker pot, pour over the hot tomato mixture, cover with the lid, and cook on high for 4–5 hours or until the potatoes are tender. Serve with warm crusty bread.

If you have any leftovers they will taste just as good the next day reheated in the microwave. Try the mixed vegetables topped with a little crumbled feta cheese and a sprinkling of arugula leaves.

$\mathcal{P}$umpkin &
parmesan gnocchi

1 tablespoon olive oil

2 tablespoons butter

1 onion, thinly sliced

2 garlic cloves, finely chopped

2 tablespoons all-purpose flour

$^2/_3$ cup dry white wine

$1^1/_4$ cups vegetable stock

2–3 stems of sage, plus extra to garnish (optional)

13 oz pumpkin (or butternut squash), seeded, peeled, diced, and weighed after preparation (about 3 cups)

1 lb chilled gnocchi

$^1/_2$ cup heavy cream

salt and pepper

freshly shaved or grated Parmesan cheese, to garnish

Preheat the slow cooker if necessary; see the manufacturer's handbook. Heat the oil and butter in a skillet, add the onion and fry, stirring, for 5 minutes or until just beginning to turn golden.

Stir in the garlic, cook for 2 minutes, then stir in the flour. Gradually mix in the wine and stock and heat, stirring until smooth. Add the sage and season well with salt and pepper.

Add the pumpkin to the slow cooker pot, pour over the hot sauce, then press the pumpkin beneath the surface of the liquid. Cover with the lid and cook on low for 6–8 hours or until the pumpkin is tender.

When almost ready to serve, bring a large saucepan of water to the boil, add the gnocchi, bring the water back to a boil and cook for 2–3 minutes or until the gnocchi float to the surface and are piping hot. Tip into a colander to drain.

Stir the cream, then the gnocchi, into the pumpkin, mix together lightly, then spoon into shallow bowls and serve topped with shaved or grated Parmesan and a few extra sage leaves, if desired.

The pumpkin sauce could also be mixed with just-cooked pasta instead of gnocchi and sprinkled with some toasted, roughly chopped hazelnuts or walnuts for a little crunch.

PREPARATION TIME **10 minutes**

COOKING TEMPERATURE **high**

COOKING TIME **4–5 hours**

SERVES **4–6**

$\mathcal{B}$raised celery
with orange

2 celery hearts

**grated zest and juice of 1 small
  orange**

2 tablespoons light brown sugar

13 oz can chopped tomatoes

salt and pepper

Preheat the slow cooker if necessary; see the manufacturer's handbook.
Cut each celery heart in half lengthwise, then rinse in cold running water
to remove any traces of dirt. Drain and put into the slow cooker pot.

Mix together the remaining ingredients and pour over the celery. Cover
with the lid and cook on high for 4–5 hours or until the celery is tender.

If you would prefer a thicker sauce, pour off the liquid from the slow
cooker pot into a saucepan and boil rapidly for 4–5 minutes to reduce.
Pour back over the celery and serve.

$\mathcal{H}$ot pickled beet

1 tablespoon olive oil

2 red onions, roughly chopped

1 bunch of beets, about 1 lb in total, trimmed, peeled, and cut into 1/2 inch cubes

1 red-skinned dessert apple, cored and diced

1 1/2 inches fresh ginger root, peeled and finely chopped

4 tablespoons red wine vinegar

2 tablespoons honey

1 3/4 cups vegetable stock

salt and pepper

TO SERVE

sour cream

dill weed

Preheat the slow cooker if necessary; see the manufacturer's handbook. Heat the oil in a skillet, add the onions and fry, stirring, for 5 minutes or until just beginning to soften and turn golden.

Stir in the beets and cook for 3 minutes, then add the apple, ginger, vinegar, and honey. Pour in the stock, add a little salt and pepper, and bring to a boil. Pour the mixture into the slow cooker pot, press the beets below the surface of the liquid, then cover with the lid and cook on low for 6–8 hours or until tender.

Serve hot as an appetizer topped with spoonfuls of sour cream and chopped dill or as a vegetable side dish.

$\mathscr{E}$ggplant timbale

4 tablespoons olive oil, plus extra
for greasing

1 large eggplant, thinly sliced

1 small onion, chopped

1 garlic clove, finely chopped

¹/₂ teaspoon ground cinnamon

¹/₄ teaspoon grated nutmeg

¹/₄ cup pistachio nuts, roughly
chopped

2 tablespoons pitted dates, roughly
chopped

2 tablespoons ready-to-eat dried
apricots, roughly chopped

¹/₃ cup easy-cook white rice

1¹/₄ cups boiling vegetable stock

salt and pepper

salad or vine tomatoes, to serve
(optional)

Preheat the slow cooker if necessary; see the manufacturer's handbook. Lightly oil the base of 2 x 1¹/₂ cup individual soufflé or straight-sided, heatproof dishes and line the base of each with a circle of nonstick parchment paper, checking first that they will fit into your slow cooker pot.

Heat 1 tablespoon oil in a skillet, add one-third of the eggplants, and fry on both sides until softened and golden. Lift out of the pan with a slotted spoon and transfer to a plate. Repeat with the rest of the eggplants using 2 more tablespoons of oil.

Heat the remaining 1 tablespoon oil in the pan, add the onion, and fry for 5 minutes or until softened. Stir in the garlic, spices, nuts, fruit, and rice. Season with salt and pepper and mix to combine.

Divide the eggplant slices into 3 piles and arrange one pile in the base of the 2 dishes, overlapping the slices. Spoon one-quarter of the rice mixture into each dish, add a second layer of eggplant slices, then divide the remaining rice equally between the dishes. Top with the remaining eggplant slices. Pour the stock into the dishes, cover with lightly oiled foil, and put in the slow cooker.

Pour boiling water into the slow cooker to come halfway up the sides of the dishes. Add the lid and cook on high for 1¹/₂–2 hours until the rice is tender.

Lift the dishes out of the slow cooker with oven mitts. Loosen the edges of the dishes with a round-bladed knife and turn out the timbales onto dinner plates. Peel off the lining paper and serve hot with a green salad or vine tomatoes.

PREPARATION TIME **15 minutes**

COOKING TEMPERATURE **high**

COOKING TIME **3–4 hours**

SERVES **4**

Tarka dhal

1¼ cups red lentils

1 onion, finely chopped

½ teaspoon turmeric

½ teaspoon cumin seeds,
   roughly crushed

¾ inch fresh ginger, root peeled and
   finely chopped

1 cup canned chopped tomatoes

2½ cups boiling vegetable stock

⅔ cup plain yogurt

salt and pepper

torn cilantro leaves, to garnish

naan bread, to serve

TARKA

1 tablespoon sunflower oil

2 teaspoons black mustard seeds

½ teaspoon cumin seeds, roughly
   crushed

pinch of turmeric

2 garlic cloves, finely chopped

Preheat the slow cooker if necessary; see the manufacturer's handbook. Rinse the lentils well with cold water, drain, and put in the slow cooker pot with the onion, spices, ginger, tomatoes, and boiling stock.

Stir in a little salt and pepper, cover with the lid, and cook on high for 3–4 hours or until the lentils are soft and tender.

When almost ready to serve, make the tarka. Heat the oil in a small skillet, add the mustard and cumin seeds, turmeric, and garlic and fry, stirring, for 2 minutes.

Roughly mash the lentil mixture and spoon it into bowls. Add spoonfuls of yogurt and drizzle with the tarka. Garnish with cilantro leaves and serve with warm naan bread.

Food for friends

Making supper in the slow cooker takes the effort out of entertaining. You know that your meal is on before your friends arrive and that the food won't spoil if you get a little delayed, so you can relax and enjoy a pre-supper drink.

$\mathcal{P}$ot-roast pheasant
with chestnuts

1 pheasant, about 1½ lb

2 tablespoons butter

1 tablespoon olive oil

7 oz shallots, halved

2 oz bacon, diced, or ready-diced pancetta

2 celery sticks, thickly sliced

1 tablespoon all-purpose flour

1¼ cups chicken stock

4 tablespoons dry sherry

3½ oz vacuum-packed prepared chestnuts

2–3 sprigs of thyme

salt and pepper

potatoes dauphinois, to serve

Preheat the slow cooker if necessary; see the manufacturer's handbook. Rinse the pheasant inside and out with plenty of cold running water and pat dry with paper towels.

Heat the butter and oil in a skillet, add the pheasant, breast side down, the shallots, bacon or pancetta, and celery and fry until golden brown, turning the pheasant and stirring the other ingredients. Transfer the pheasant to the slow cooker pot, placing it breast side down.

Stir the flour into the onion mix. Gradually add the stock and sherry, then add the chestnuts, thyme, and a little salt and pepper. Bring to a boil, stirring, then spoon over the pheasant. Cover with the lid and cook on high for 3–4 hours until tender. Test with a knife through the thickest part of the pheasant leg and breast to make sure that the juices run clear.

Carve the pheasant breast into slices and cut the legs away from the body. Serve with potatoes dauphinois.

Chermoula salmon

6 scallions

¹/₂ cup parsley

1 cup cilantro

grated zest and juice of 1 lemon

4 tablespoons olive oil

¹/₂ teaspoon cumin seeds, roughly crushed

1 lb thick end salmon fillet, no longer than 7 inches, skinned

1 cup fish stock

6 tablespoons mayonnaise

2¹/₂ cups mixed salad leaves

salt and pepper

Preheat the slow cooker if necessary; see the manufacturer's handbook. Finely chop the scallions and herbs with a large knife or in a food processor. Mix with the lemon zest and juice, the oil, cumin seeds, and a little salt and pepper.

Rinse the salmon with cold water, drain well, and place on a long piece of kitchen foil, the width of the salmon. Press half the herb mixture over both sides of the salmon, then use the foil to lower the fish into the slow cooker pot.

Bring the stock to a boil in a small saucepan, pour over the salmon and tuck the ends of the foil down if needed. Cover with the lid and cook on low for 1³/₄–2¹/₄ hours or until the fish flakes into opaque pieces when pressed in the center with a knife.

Use the foil to lift the salmon out of the slow cooker pot and transfer to a serving plate. Mix the remaining uncooked herb mixture with the mayonnaise. Arrange the salad leaves on 4 plates. Cut the salmon into 4 pieces and place on the salad. Serve with the herb mayonnaise.

For heartier appetites, toss some thickly sliced, cooked new potatoes with the herb mayonnaise, spoon into the center of the plates, then top with salad leaves and salmon.

PREPARATION TIME **20 minutes**

COOKING TEMPERATURE **low and high**

COOKING TIME **6¹/₄–8¹/₄ hours**

SERVES **4**

*G*reen chicken curry

1 tablespoon sunflower oil

2 tablespoons Thai green curry paste

2 teaspoons galangal paste

2 Thai green chilies, seeded and
thinly sliced

1 onion, finely chopped

8 chicken thighs, about 2 lb in total,
skinned, boned, and cubed

1³/₄ cups full-fat coconut milk

²/₃ cup chicken stock

4 dried kaffir lime leaves

2 teaspoons light brown sugar

2 teaspoons Thai fish sauce
(nam pla)

4 oz sugar snap peas

4 oz green beans, halved

small bunch of cilantro, to garnish

rice, to serve

Preheat the slow cooker if necessary; see the manufacturer's handbook.
Heat the oil in a skillet, add the curry paste, galangal paste, and green
chilies and cook for 1 minute.

Stir in the onion and chicken and cook, stirring, until the chicken is
just beginning to turn golden. Pour in the coconut milk and stock, then
add the lime leaves, sugar, and fish sauce. Bring to a boil, stirring.

Transfer the mixture to the slow cooker pot, cover with the lid, and
cook on low for 6–8 hours or until the chicken is tender.

Stir in the peas and beans and cook on high for 15 minutes or until they
are just tender. Tear the cilantro leaves over the top, spoon into bowls,
and serve with rice.

Thai curry paste and fish sauce are now
widely available in all of the larger
supermarkets. Galangal paste is sold in
small jars and has a gingery taste, while
dried kaffir lime leaves can also be found
in jars in the same section.

Venison puff pie

2 tablespoons butter

1 tablespoon olive oil

1½ lb diced venison

1 onion, chopped

2 tablespoons all-purpose flour

¾ cup red wine

1 cup lamb or beef stock

3 raw medium beets, peeled and cut into ½ inch dice

1 tablespoon red currant jelly

1 tablespoon tomato paste

10 juniper berries, roughly crushed

3 sprigs of thyme

1 bay leaf

1 sheet, about 7 oz, prepared puff pastry

beaten egg, for glazing

salt and pepper

roasted parsnips and baby carrots, to serve

Preheat the slow cooker if necessary; see the manufacturer's handbook. Heat the butter and oil in a skillet, add the venison a few pieces at a time until all the pieces are in the pan, then fry, stirring, until evenly browned. Scoop the venison out of the pan with a slotted spoon and transfer to the slow cooker pot.

Add the onion to the pan juices and fry for 5 minutes until softened. Stir in the flour, then mix in the wine and stock. Add the beets, red currant jelly and tomato paste, then the juniper, 2 sprigs of thyme, and the bay leaf. Season with a little salt and pepper and bring to a boil.

Pour the sauce over the venison, cover with the lid, and cook on low for 8–10 hours.

About 30 minutes before you are ready to serve, unroll the pastry, trim the edges to make an oval similar in size to the slow cooker pot. Transfer to a greased baking sheet and flute the edges. Cut leaves from the trimmings and add to pie lid. Brush with egg, sprinkle with the remaining thyme leaves torn from the stem and coarse salt, and bake in a preheated oven, 425°F, for about 20 minutes until well risen and golden.

Stir the venison and spoon onto serving plates. Cut the pastry into portions and place on top of the venison. Serve with roasted parsnips and baby carrots.

For a gourmet-style shepherd's pie the venison could be topped with creamy mashed potato flavored with garlic, horseradish, and chopped chives.

Caribbean trout stew

4 small trout, gutted, heads and fins removed and rinsed well with cold water

1 teaspoon ground allspice

1 teaspoon paprika

1 teaspoon ground coriander

2 tablespoons olive oil

6 scallions, thickly sliced

1 red bell pepper, cored, seeded, and thinly sliced

2 tomatoes, roughly chopped

½ red hot bonnet or other red chili, seeded and chopped

2 sprigs of thyme

1¼ cups fish stock

salt and pepper

bread, to serve (optional)

Preheat the slow cooker if necessary; see the manufacturer's handbook. Slash the trout on each side 2–3 times with a sharp knife. Mix the spices and a little salt and pepper on a plate and dip each side of the trout in the spice mix.

Heat the oil in a skillet, add the trout and fry until browned on both sides but not cooked all the way through. Drain and arrange in the slow cooker pot with the fish resting on their lower edges and top to tailing them so that they fit snugly in a single layer.

Add the remaining ingredients to the skillet with any spices left on the plate and bring to a boil, stirring. Pour over the trout, then cover with the lid and cook on high for 1½–2 hours or until the fish breaks into flakes when pressed in the center with a knife.

Use a spatula to lift the fish carefully out of the slow cooker pot and transfer to shallow dishes. Spoon over the sauce and serve with warm bread to mop up the sauce, if desired.

The blend of spices used in this dish is typical of Caribbean fish cookery and although traditionally it would be wrapped in foil and barbecued, it tastes just as good prepared in the slow cooker.

Chinese duck

4 duck legs, each about 7 oz

1 onion, sliced

2 tablespoons all-purpose flour

1³/4 cups chicken stock

2 tablespoons soy sauce

1 tablespoon red wine vinegar

1 tablespoon honey

2 teaspoons tomato paste

2 teaspoons Thai fish sauce
    (nam pla)

¹/2 teaspoon crushed red pepper

¹/2 teaspoon ground allspice

4 star anise

12 oz red plums, pitted and
    quartered

rice or gingered noodles, to serve

Preheat the slow cooker if necessary; see the manufacturer's handbook. Dry-fry the duck legs in a skillet over a low heat until the fat begins to run, then increase the heat and brown on both sides. Lift them out of the pan with a slotted spoon and transfer to the slow cooker pot.

Pour off all but 1 tablespoon of the duck fat from the pan, then add the onion and fry, stirring, for 5 minutes or until just turning golden. Stir in the flour, then gradually mix in the stock. Add all the remaining ingredients, except the plums, and bring to a boil, stirring.

Pour the sauce over the duck, add the plums, and press the duck beneath the surface of the liquid. Cover with the lid and cook on high for 5–6 hours or until the duck is almost falling off the bones. Serve with rice or with gingered noodles.

To make gingered noodles heat 1 tablespoon sesame oil in a wok, add 1 inch finely chopped fresh ginger root, 3 cups finely shredded bok choy, ¹/2 cup snow peas, halved, and 14¹/2 oz, straight-to-wok noodles. Stir-fry for 3–4 minutes.

$\mathcal{S}$almon-wrapped cod
with buttered leeks

2 cod loins, about 1½ lb in total

juice of 1 lemon

4 stems of dill, plus extra to garnish (optional)

4 slices of smoked salmon, about 6 oz in total

1 leek, thinly sliced; white and green parts kept separate

4 tablespoons Noilly Prat or dry white wine

¾ cup boiling fish stock

2 teaspoons drained capers (optional)

⅓ cup butter, diced

2 tablespoons chopped chives or parsley

salt and pepper

baby new potatoes, to serve (optional)

Preheat the slow cooker if necessary; see the manufacturer's handbook. Cut each cod loin in half to give 4 portions, then drizzle with the lemon juice and season with salt and pepper. Add a dill stem to the top of each portion, then wrap with a slice of smoked salmon.

Put the white leek slices into the base of the slow cooker pot, arrange the fish on top in a single layer, tilting them slightly so that they rest slightly at an angle if necessary to make them fit. Add the Noilly Prat and hot stock, then cover and cook on low for 1½–2 hours or until a knife pressed into the center of one of the fish steaks flakes easily into white pieces.

Carefully lift out the fish with a spatula and put it on a warm serving plate. Cover with foil and keep hot. Pour the white leeks and cooking juices from the slow cooker into a saucepan, add the green leek slices and the capers (if used), and boil rapidly for about 5 minutes until the liquid is reduced to 4–6 tablespoons. Scoop out and reserve the leeks as soon as the green slices have softened.

Gradually beat in the butter, a piece at a time until melted, and continue until all the butter has been added and the sauce is smooth and glossy. Return the cooked leeks to the sauce with the chopped herbs and check the seasoning.

Arrange the fish in the center of 4 serving plates, then spoon the sauce around. Garnish with extra dill and serve with a separate bowl of baby new potatoes, if desired.

*M*inted lamb
with beet couscous

1 tablespoon olive oil

½ shoulder of lamb, 1 lb 14 oz–2 lb

1 onion, sliced

2 garlic cloves, finely chopped

2 tablespoons all-purpose flour

3 tablespoons mint jelly

⅔ cup red wine

1¼ cups lamb stock

salt and pepper

HERBY COUSCOUS

1 cup couscous

3 cooked beets, about 5 oz, peeled and diced

1¾ cups boiling water

grated zest and juice of 1 lemon

2 tablespoons olive oil

small bunch of parsley, finely chopped

small bunch of mint, finely chopped

Preheat the slow cooker if necessary; see the manufacturer's handbook. Heat the oil in a skillet, add the lamb, and fry on both sides until browned. Lift out with 2 slotted spoons and transfer to the slow cooker pot. Fry the onion, stirring, for 5 minutes or until softened and just turning golden.

Stir in the garlic, then the flour. Add the mint jelly and wine and mix until smooth. Pour in the stock, season with salt and pepper, and bring to a boil, stirring. Pour the sauce over the lamb, cover with the lid, and cook on high for 7–8 hours or until the lamb is almost falling off the bone.

When almost ready to serve, put the couscous and beet in a bowl, pour over the boiling water, then add the lemon zest and juice, oil, and some salt and pepper. Cover with a plate and allow to soak for 5 minutes.

Add the herbs to the couscous and fluff up with a fork, then spoon onto plates. Lift the lamb onto a serving dish and carve into rough pieces, discarding the bone. Arrange on the plates and serve the sauce separately in a pitcher.

Tarragon chicken

1 tablespoon olive oil

1 tablespoon butter

4 boneless, skinless chicken breasts, about 1 lb 6 oz in total

7 oz shallots, halved

1 tablespoon all-purpose flour

1¼ cups chicken stock

4 tablespoons dry vermouth

2 sprigs of tarragon, plus extra to serve

3 tablespoons heavy cream

2 tablespoons chopped chives

salt and pepper

coarsely mashed potatoes mixed with peas, to serve (optional)

Preheat the slow cooker if necessary; see the manufacturer's handbook. Heat the oil and butter in a skillet, add the chicken, and fry over a high heat until golden on both sides but not cooked through. Drain and arrange in the slow cooker pot in a single layer.

Add the shallots to the skillet and cook, stirring, for 4–5 minutes or until just beginning to turn golden. Stir in the flour, then gradually mix in the stock and vermouth. Add the sprigs of tarragon, a little salt and pepper and bring to the boil, stirring.

Pour the sauce over the chicken, cover with the lid, and cook on high for 3–4 hours or until the chicken is cooked through to the center.

Stir the cream into the sauce and sprinkle over 1 tablespoon chopped tarragon and the chives. Serve with coarsely mashed potatoes mixed with peas.

This is a good basic recipe to adapt to suit what you have in your refrigerator. You could substitute a chopped onion or 4 scallions for the shallots and sherry or wine for the vermouth. Try pesto or 1 teaspoon of Dijon mustard instead of the tarragon.

PREPARATION TIME **20 minutes**

COOKING TEMPERATURE **high**

COOKING TIME **7–9 hours**

SERVES **4**

$\mathscr{S}$low-braised pork
with ratatouille

1 tablespoon olive oil

1 onion, chopped

1 red bell pepper, cored, seeded, and cut into chunks

1 yellow bell pepper, cored, seeded, and cut into chunks

2 zucchini, about 12 oz, cut into chunks

2 garlic cloves, finely chopped

13 oz can chopped tomatoes

²/₃ cup red wine or chicken stock

1 tablespoon cornstarch

2–3 stems of rosemary, leaves torn from the sprigs

1¾ lb piece thick end pork belly, rind and any string removed

salt and pepper

mashed potatoes, to serve

Preheat the slow cooker if necessary; see the manufacturer's handbook. Heat the oil in a skillet, add the onion and fry, stirring, for 5 minutes or until just beginning to turn golden.

Add the peppers, zucchini, and garlic and fry for 2 minutes, then mix in the tomatoes and the wine or stock. Mix the cornstarch to a smooth paste with a little water, then stir into the pan with the rosemary leaves and some salt and pepper. Bring to a boil, stirring.

Pour half the mixture into the slow cooker pot, add the unrolled pork belly and cover with the rest of the vegetable mixture. Cover with the lid and cook on high for 7–9 hours or until the pork is almost falling apart.

If you like a thick sauce, ladle the juices out of the slow cooker pot into a saucepan and boil for 5 minutes to reduce. Cut the pork into 4 pieces, then spoon into shallow dishes and serve with mashed potatoes and the tomato sauce.

Pork belly is available in one piece in some supermarkets, but this is a cut that is best bought from a specialty butcher. Remember to ask for the "thickest" part of pork belly as this will be leaner and meatier.

Rogan josh

2 tablespoons butter

1½ lb boned rib of lamb, sliced

2 onions, chopped

3 garlic cloves, finely chopped

1 inch fresh ginger root, peeled and finely chopped

1 teaspoon ground turmeric

2 teaspoons ground coriander

2 teaspoons cumin seeds, roughly crushed

2 teaspoons garam masala

½ teaspoon crushed red pepper

2 tablespoons all-purpose flour

13 oz can chopped tomatoes

1¼ cups lamb stock

4 tablespoons heavy cream

TO GARNISH

small bunch of cilantro, leaves torn

red onion, thinly sliced

TO SERVE

pilau rice

naan bread

Preheat the slow cooker if necessary; see the manufacturer's handbook. Heat the butter in a skillet, add the lamb a few pieces at a time until all the meat is in the pan, then fry, stirring, over a high heat until browned. Lift out of the pan with a slotted spoon and transfer to the slow cooker pot.

Add the onions to the pan and fry, stirring, for 5 minutes or until softened and just beginning to turn golden. Stir in the garlic, ginger, spices, and crushed pepper and cook for 1 minute. Mix in the flour, then add the tomatoes and stock. Bring to a boil, stirring.

Pour the tomato mixture over the lamb, cover with the lid, and cook on low for 8–10 hours or until the lamb is tender. Stir in the cream, garnish with the torn cilantro leaves and red onion, and serve with pilau rice and naan bread.

PREPARATION TIME **15 minutes**

COOKING TEMPERATURE **high**

COOKING TIME **5–7 hours**

SERVES **4**

$\mathcal{L}$amb shanks
with juniper

2 tablespoons butter

4 lamb shanks, about 3 lb in total

2 small red onions, cut into wedges

2 tablespoons all-purpose flour

¾ cup red wine

1¾ cups lamb stock

2 tablespoons cranberry sauce
  (optional)

1 tablespoon tomato paste

2 bay leaves

1 teaspoon juniper berries,
  roughly crushed

1 small cinnamon stick, halved

pared rind of 1 small orange

salt and pepper

TO SERVE

mashed sweet potatoes

green beans

Preheat the slow cooker if necessary; see the manufacturer's handbook. Heat the butter in a skillet, add the lamb shanks, and fry over a medium heat, turning until browned all over. Drain and put into the slow cooker pot.

Add the onions to the pan and fry for 4–5 minutes or until just beginning to turn golden. Stir in the flour. Gradually mix in the wine and stock, then add the cranberry sauce (if used) and the remaining ingredients. Bring to a boil, stirring.

Transfer the mixture to the slow cooker pot, cover with the lid, and cook on high for 5–7 hours or until the lamb is beginning to fall off the bone. If you like thick sauces, pour the sauce into a pan and boil rapidly for 5 minutes or until reduced by one-third. Serve the lamb with mashed sweet potatoes and green beans.

Desserts

The slow cooker is perfect for getting organized. You can bake and chill a custard-style dessert or fruit compote or put on a hot pudding well in advance and then relax. It won't matter if the main course takes longer than you'd planned— just dish up when you're ready.

$\mathscr{S}$affron pears
with chocolate

1¼ cups cloudy apple juice

3 tablespoons superfine sugar

large pinch of saffron threads

4 cardamom pods, roughly crushed

4 firm, ripe pears

CHOCOLATE SAUCE

4 tablespoons chocolate and hazelnut
spread

2 tablespoons heavy cream

2 tablespoons milk

Preheat the slow cooker if necessary; see the manufacturer's handbook. Pour the apple juice into a small saucepan, add the sugar, saffron, and cardamom pods and their tiny black seeds. Bring to a boil, then tip into the slow cooker pot.

Cut each pear in half lengthwise, leaving the stalk on, then cut away the skin. Remove the pear cores with a melon baller, if you have one, or a teaspoon. Add the pears to the slow cooker pot, pressing them beneath the surface of the liquid as much as you can. Cover with the lid and cook on low for 3–4 hours or until the pears are tender and pale yellow.

When you are almost ready to serve, put all the ingredients for the sauce into a small saucepan and warm together, stirring until smooth. Spoon the pears and some of the saffron sauce into shallow dishes, then pour the chocolate sauce into a small pitcher to allow your guests to drizzle the sauce over the pears just before eating.

PREPARATION TIME **20 minutes**

COOKING TEMPERATURE **high**

COOKING TIME **1¼–1½ hours**

SERVES **4**

Chocolate puddings

4 oz semisweet chocolate, plus
    8 extra small squares

⅓ cup butter

2 eggs

2 egg yolks

⅓ cup superfine sugar

½ teaspoon vanilla extract

6 tablespoons all-purpose flour

sifted confectioners' sugar, to
    decorate

TO SERVE

mini marshmallows

vanilla ice cream or sour cream

Preheat the slow cooker if necessary; see the manufacturer's handbook. Break the 4 oz chocolate into pieces, put them into a saucepan with the butter, and heat gently, stirring occasionally, until melted. Take off the heat and set aside.

Beat together the whole eggs, egg yolks, sugar, and vanilla extract in a large bowl with an electric mixer for 3–4 minutes or until light and frothy. Gradually beat in the melted chocolate mixture.

Sift the flour into the chocolate mix and fold together. Pour into 4 x 1 cup buttered and base-lined individual metal pudding molds. Press 2 squares of chocolate into the center of each one, then loosely cover the tops with squares of buttered foil.

Transfer the pudding molds to the slow cooker pot and pour boiling water into the pot to come halfway up the sides of the molds. Cover with the lid and cook on high for 1¼–1½ hours until well risen and the pudding tops spring back when lightly pressed.

Loosen the puddings with a knife, turn out into shallow serving dishes, and remove the lining paper. Sprinkle with sifted confectioners' sugar and serve with marshmallows and spoonfuls of vanilla ice cream or sour cream.

Crème caramels

butter, for greasing

½ cup granulated sugar

½ cup water

2 tablespoons boiling water

2 eggs

3 egg yolks

13 oz can sweetened condensed milk

½ cup lowfat milk

grated zest of ½ small lemon

Preheat the slow cooker if necessary; see the manufacturer's handbook. Lightly butter 4 x 1 cup individual metal pudding molds. Pour the sugar and water into a small saucepan and heat gently, stirring occasionally until the sugar has completely dissolved.

Increase the heat and boil the syrup for 5 minutes, without stirring, until it has turned golden, keeping a watchful eye as it cooks. Take the pan off the heat, add the boiling water, and stand well back.

Tilt the pan to mix, and when the bubbles have subsided pour the caramel sauce into the pudding molds, tilting them so that the syrup coats the base and sides.

Put the eggs and egg yolks into a bowl and fork together. Pour the condensed milk and fresh milk into a saucepan, bring to a boil, then gradually beat into the egg mixture until smooth. Strain back into the pan, then stir in the lemon zest.

Pour the custard into the syrup-lined pudding molds, then transfer the molds to the slow cooker pot. Cover the top of each mold with a square of foil. Pour hot water around the molds so that the water comes halfway up the sides, then cover with the lid and cook on low for 2½–3½ hours or until the custard is set with just a slight wobble in the center.

If you haven't made caramel sauce before resist the urge to stir it once it is boiling or you may find that the sauce crystallizes before it has a chance to brown.

Lift the molds out of the slow cooker pot with a dishtowel, allow to cool, then transfer to the refrigerator for 3–4 hours or overnight to chill.

To serve, dip the base of the molds into boiling water for 10 seconds, loosen the top of the custard with a fingertip, then turn out onto rimmed plates.

PREPARATION TIME **30 minutes, plus chilling**

COOKING TEMPERATURE **high**

COOKING TIME **2–2½ hours**

SERVES **4–5**

Strawberry cheesecake

4 pieces of sponge cake

1¼ cups full-fat cream cheese

⅓ cup superfine sugar

⅔ cup heavy cream

3 eggs

grated zest and juice of ½ lemon

TOPPING

2 tablespoons strawberry jelly

1 tablespoon lemon juice

1¼ cups strawberries, hulled
    and sliced

Preheat the slow cooker if necessary; see the manufacturer's handbook. Use nonstick parchment paper to line the base and sides of a soufflé dish that is 5½ inches in diameter and 3½ inches high. Line the base with the sponge cake, trimming to fit in an even layer.

Put the cream cheese and sugar in a bowl, then gradually beat in the cream until smooth and thick. Gradually beat in the eggs one at a time, then mix in the lemon zest and juice.

Pour the cream cheese mixture into the prepared dish and spread level. Cover the top of the dish loosely with buttered foil and lower it into the slow cooker pot with foil straps (see page 17). Pour boiling water into the pot to come halfway up the sides of the dish.

Cover with the lid and cook on high for 2–2½ hours until the cheesecake is puffy and well risen and softly set in the middle. Take the dish out of the slow cooker and allow to cool and firm up. The cheesecake will sink quickly as it cools to about the size that it was before cooking. When it is cool, transfer to the refrigerator for 4 hours or overnight.

When ready to serve, loosen the edges of the cheesecake with a round-bladed knife, turn it out, peel off the paper, and turn it the right way up. Put it on a serving plate. Mix the jelly and lemon juice in a bowl until smooth, add the sliced strawberries and toss together. Spoon on top of the cheesecake and serve immediately.

Choose whatever fruits are in season. We used sliced strawberries, but you could use mixed berry fruits or diced peaches and raspberries if you prefer.

PREPARATION TIME **10 minutes**

COOKING TEMPERATURE **low**

COOKING TIME **2½–3 hours**

SERVES **4**

*H*oneyed rice pudding

butter for greasing

3 cups whole milk

3 tablespoons honey

½ cup risotto rice

TO SERVE

jelly

thick cream

Preheat the slow cooker if necessary; see the manufacturer's handbook. Lightly butter the inside of the slow cooker pot.

Pour the milk into a saucepan, add the honey, and bring just to a boil, stirring until the honey has melted. Pour into the slow cooker pot, add the rice and stir gently.

Cover with the lid and cook on low for 2½–3 hours, stirring once during cooking, or until the pudding is thickened and the rice is soft. Stir again just before spooning into dishes and serve topped with spoonfuls of jelly (or the apricot conserve on page 224) and thick cream.

PREPARATION TIME **20 minutes**

COOKING TEMPERATURE **low**

COOKING TIME **3–4 hours**

SERVES **4**

$\mathcal{B}$aked apples
with dates

¼ cup butter at room temperature

¼ cup light brown sugar

½ teaspoon ground cinnamon

grated zest of ½ small orange

1 tablespoon finely chopped candied or drained stem ginger

⅓ cup ready-chopped pitted dates

4 large, firm dessert apples, such as Braeburn

⅔ cup cloudy apple juice

custard or cream, to serve

Preheat the slow cooker if necessary; see the manufacturer's handbook. Mix together the butter, sugar, cinnamon, and orange zest until smooth, then stir in the chopped ginger and dates.

Trim a thin slice off the bottom of the apples, if needed, so that they will stand up without rolling over, then cut a thick slice off the top of each and reserve for later. Using a small knife, cut away the apple core to leave a cavity for the stuffing.

Divide the date mixture into 4 and press a portion into each apple cavity, spreading it over the top cut edge of the apple if it won't all fit in. Replace the apple lids and put the apples into the slow cooker pot. Pour the apple juice into the base of the pot, cover with the lid, and cook on low for 3–4 hours or until the apples are tender.

Lift the apples carefully out of the slow cooker and serve in shallow dishes with the sauce spooned over and a drizzle of hot custard or cream.

$\mathscr{S}$ticky marmalade
syrup pudding

4 tablespoons light corn syrup

3 tablespoons orange marmalade

1¹⁄₂ cups self-rising flour

³⁄₄ cup shredded vegetable suet

¹⁄₄ cup light brown sugar

1 teaspoon ground ginger

grated zest and juice of 1 orange

2 eggs

2 tablespoons milk

custard or vanilla ice cream, to serve

Preheat the slow cooker if necessary; see the manufacturer's handbook. Lightly butter a 5 cup pudding mold (checking first that it will fit into your slow cooker pot) and line the base with a circle of nonstick parchment paper. Spoon the corn syrup and 2 tablespoons of the marmalade into the pot.

Put the flour, suet, sugar, and ginger in a bowl and mix together. Add the remaining marmalade, orange zest and juice, the eggs, and milk and beat until smooth.

Spoon the mixture into the pudding mold, level the surface, and cover the top of the basin with a piece of buttered foil. Lower into the slow cooker pot, using foil straps or string (see page 17). Pour boiling water into the pot to come halfway up the sides of the mold.

Cover with the lid and cook on high for 3–3¹⁄₂ hours or until the pudding is well risen and feels firm and dry when the top is pressed with a fingertip.

Lift the basin out of the slow cooker with oven mitts, remove the foil and loosen the edge of the pudding with a round-bladed knife. Invert the mold on a plate, remove the mold, and peel off the lining paper. Serve scoops of the pudding with custard or vanilla ice cream.

This pudding is delicious served drizzled with fresh or canned custard, especially if it's flavored with a few tablespoons of sherry, Grand Marnier, or Cointreau.

$\mathcal{J}$ced Jamaican
ginger cake

¹/₂ cup butter, plus extra for greasing

¹/₂ cup dark brown sugar

¹/₃ cup light corn syrup

²/₃ cup ready-chopped pitted dates

²/₃ cup whole-wheat all-purpose flour

1 cup self-rising flour

¹/₂ teaspoon baking soda

2 teaspoons ground ginger

3 pieces of stem ginger, drained , 2 chopped and 1 cut into strips

2 eggs, beaten

6 tablespoons milk

1 cup confectioners' sugar, sifted

3–3¹/₂ teaspoons water

Preheat the slow cooker if necessary; see the manufacturer's handbook. Butter a soufflé dish that is 5¹/₂ inches in diameter and 3¹/₂ inches high and base-line with a circle of nonstick parchment paper.

Put the measured butter, sugar, syrup, and dates into a saucepan and heat gently, stirring, until the butter and sugar have melted. Take the pan off the heat, add the flours, baking soda, ground and chopped ginger, eggs, and milk and beat until smooth. Pour into the lined dish and cover the top loosely with buttered foil.

Lower the dish carefully into the slow cooker pot on foil straps (see page 17) or tie string around the top edge of the dish. Pour boiling water into the pot to come halfway up the sides of the dish, cover with the lid, and cook on high for 4¹/₂–5 hours or until a skewer comes out cleanly when inserted into the center of the ginger cake.

Take the dish out of the slow cooker pot, allow to stand for 10 minutes, then remove the foil and loosen the edge of the cake with a round-bladed knife. Turn out the cake on a wire rack, peel off the lining paper and allow to cool.

Sift the confectioners' sugar into a bowl and mix in just enough water to make a smooth, thick icing. Spoon over the top of the cake, then decorate with the strips of ginger. Allow to set. Cut the cake into wedges to serve.

PREPARATION TIME **30 minutes, plus chilling**

COOKING TEMPERATURE **low**

COOKING TIME **2½–3½ hours**

SERVES **4**

Peppermint
& raspberry brûlée

4 egg yolks

3 tablespoons superfine sugar

1¾ cups heavy cream

¼ teaspoon peppermint extract

1¼ cups raspberries

2 tablespoons confectioners' sugar

mint leaves, to decorate (optional)

Preheat the slow cooker if necessary; see the manufacturer's handbook. Beat the egg yolks and sugar in a bowl for 3–4 minutes until frothy, then gradually beat in the cream.

Stir in the peppermint extract then strain the egg custard into a pitcher. Pour into 4 x ⅔ cup ramekin dishes.

Put the dishes into the slow cooker pot, pour hot water into the pot to come halfway up the sides of the dishes, then loosely cover the top of each dish with foil. Cook on low for 2½–3½ hours or until the custard is set with a slight quiver to the center.

Carefully lift the dishes out of the slow cooker, allow to cool then transfer to the refrigerator for 4 hours to chill.

When ready to serve, pile a few raspberries in the center of each dish and sprinkle over some confectioners' sugar. Caramelize the sugar with a kitchen torch and decorate with a few tiny mint leaves, if desired.

If you don't have a kitchen torch, pop the ramekins under a preheated hot broiler instead. Omit the raspberries, sprinkle the dishes with sugar and put in a roasting pan with ice so that the custards stay cold as the sugar topping melts and caramelizes.

PREPARATION TIME **20 minutes**

COOKING TEMPERATURE **high**

COOKING TIME **2–2½ hours**

SERVES **4**

$\mathcal{P}$ineapple
upside-down puddings

butter, for greasing

4 tablespoons light corn syrup

2 tablespoons light brown sugar

7½ oz can pineapple rings, drained
   and chopped

3 tablespoons candied cherries,
   roughly chopped

custard, to serve (optional)

BATTER

¼ cup butter at room temperature
   or soft margarine

¼ cup superfine sugar

½ cup self-rising flour

⅓ cup shredded coconut

1 egg

1 tablespoon milk

Preheat the slow cooker if necessary; see the manufacturer's handbook. Lightly butter 4 x 1 cup individual metal pudding molds and base-line with a circle of nonstick parchment paper. Add 1 tablespoon corn syrup and ½ tablespoon sugar to the base of each, then add three-quarters of the pineapple and all the cherries.

Make the batter. Put all the ingredients for the batter and the remaining pineapple into a bowl and beat together until smooth. Spoon the mixture into the pudding molds. Level the surface with the back of a small spoon, then cover the top of each mold loosely with buttered foil.

Stand the molds in the slow cooker pot, then pour boiling water into the pot to come halfway up the sides of the molds. Cover with the lid and cook on high for 2–2½ hours or until the puddings are well risen and spring back when pressed with a fingertip.

Remove the foil, loosen the edges of the puddings with a round-bladed knife and turn out into shallow bowls. Peel away the lining paper and serve with hot custard, if desired.

Add a couple of tablespoons of your favorite canned fruit pie filling to the base of the molds, adding a little grated orange zest to the batter instead of the pineapple.

$\mathscr{H}$ot toddy oranges

8 clementines

1¹/₂ tablespoons honey

¹/₃ cup light brown sugar

grated zest and juice of ¹/₂ lemon

4 tablespoons whiskey

1¹/₄ cups boiling water

1 tablespoon butter

ice cream, to serve

Preheat the slow cooker if necessary; see the manufacturer's handbook. Peel the clementines but leave them whole.

Place the remaining ingredients in the slow cooker pot and mix together. Add the oranges. Cover with the lid and cook on low for 2–3 hours until piping hot.

Spoon into shallow dishes and serve with just-melting scoops of vanilla ice cream.

This warming winter pudding can also be made with 4 large oranges instead of clementines. Peel and cut them into horizontal slices or divide into segments, if preferred.

PREPARATION TIME **25 minutes**

COOKING TEMPERATURE **high**

COOKING TIME **4½–5 hours**

SERVES **6–8**

$\mathcal{L}$emon & poppy seed
drizzle cake

½ cup butter at room temperature,
   plus extra for greasing

½ cup superfine sugar

2 eggs, beaten

1 cup self-rising flour

2 tablespoons poppy seeds

grated zest of 1 lemon

sour cream, to serve

lemon rind curls, to decorate

LEMON SYRUP

juice of 1½ lemons

½ cup superfine sugar

Preheat the slow cooker if necessary; see the manufacturer's handbook. Lightly butter a soufflé dish that is 5½ inches in diameter and 3½ inches high, and base-line it with a circle of nonstick parchment paper.

Cream together the measured butter and sugar in a bowl with a wooden spoon or electric hand mixer. Gradually mix in alternate spoonfuls of beaten egg and flour and continue adding and beating until the mixture is smooth. Stir in the poppy seeds and lemon zest, then spoon the mixture into the soufflé dish and level the top. Cover the top of the dish loosely with buttered foil and then lower into the slow cooker pot using foil straps (see page 17).

Pour boiling water into the slow cooker pot so that it comes halfway up the sides of the dish. Cover with the lid and cook on high for 4½–5 hours or until the cake is dry and springs back when pressed with a fingertip.

Lift the dish carefully out of the slow cooker with a dishtowel, remove the foil and loosen the edge of the cake with a round-bladed knife. Turn out onto a plate or shallow dish with a rim and remove the lining paper.

Quickly warm together the lemon juice and sugar for the syrup and pour the syrup over the cake as soon as the sugar has dissolved. Allow to cool and the syrup to soak in. Cut into slices and serve with spoonfuls of sour cream, decorated with lemon rind curls.

PREPARATION TIME **20 minutes**

COOKING TEMPERATURE **high**

COOKING TIME **7–8 hours**

REHEATING TIME **2–2½ hours**

SERVES **6–8**

Christmas pudding

butter, for greasing

4½ cups mixed luxury dried fruit, larger fruits diced

½ cup pistachio nuts, roughly chopped

3 tablespoons finely chopped candied or stem ginger

1 dessert apple, peeled, cored, and coarsely grated

grated zest and juice of 1 lemon

grated zest and juice of 1 orange

4 tablespoons brandy

¼ cup dark brown sugar

½ cup self-rising flour

1½ cups bread crumbs

1 cup vegetable suet

1 teaspoon ground mixed spice

2 eggs, beaten

TO SERVE

4 tablespoons brandy (optional)

brandy butter or cream

Preheat the slow cooker if necessary; see the manufacturer's handbook. Check that a 6 cup pudding mold will fit inside your slow cooker pot with a little room to spare, then butter the inside of the mold and base-line with a circle of nonstick parchment paper.

Put the dried fruit, nuts, ginger, and grated apple into a large bowl. Add the fruit zests and juice and brandy and mix together well. Stir in the remaining ingredients. Spoon into the buttered mold, pressing down well as you go. Cover with a large circle of nonstick baking paper, then a piece of foil. Tie with string and add a string handle.

Lower into the slow cooker pot, using string handles (see page 17) and pour boiling water into the pot to come two-thirds up the sides of the mold. Cover with the lid and cook on high for 7–8 hours. Check halfway through cooking and top up with extra boiling water if needed. Take the pudding out of the slow cooker with a dishtowel and allow to cool.

Cover the pudding with fresh foil, leaving the parchment paper in place. Fasten with string and keep in a cool place for 2 months or until Christmas.

To serve, preheat the slow cooker if necessary, add the pudding and boiling water as above and reheat on high for 2–2½ hours. Remove the foil and paper, loosen the pudding and turn it out. Warm the brandy (if used) in a saucepan. When it is just boiling, flame with a taper and quickly pour over the pudding. Serve with brandy butter or cream.

Winter berry compote

1¼ cups cranberries

1 lb red plums, quartered and pitted

1¼ cups red seedless grapes, halved

4 teaspoons cornstarch

1¼ cups red grape juice

6 tablespoons superfine sugar

1 cinnamon stick, halved

pared rind of 1 small orange

LEMON CURD CREAM

⅔ cup heavy cream, lightly whipped

3 tablespoons lemon curd

Preheat the slow cooker if necessary; see the manufacturer's handbook. Put the cranberries, plums, and grapes into the slow cooker pot.

Mix the cornstarch with a little of the grape juice in a bowl until smooth, then stir in the remaining juice. Pour into the slow cooker pot and add the sugar, cinnamon, and orange rind. Stir together, then cover with the lid and cook on low for 2½–3½ hours or until the fruit is tender.

Stir the compote, discard the cinnamon, and serve warm or cold spooned into bowls and topped with the Lemon Curd Cream, if desired.

PREPARATION TIME **10 minutes**

COOKING TEMPERATURE **low**

COOKING TIME **1¹/₂–2 hours**

SERVES **4**

$\mathscr{S}$ticky rum bananas
with vanilla

2 tablespoons butter

¹/₃ cup light brown sugar

grated zest and juice of 1 lime

1 vanilla bean or 1 teaspoon vanilla
    extract

3 tablespoons white or dark rum

³/₄ cup boiling water

6 small bananas, peeled and halved
    lengthwise

curls of lime rind, to decorate

vanilla ice cream, to serve (optional)

Preheat the slow cooker if necessary; see the manufacturer's handbook.
Add the butter, sugar, and lime zest and juice to the slow cooker pot as it
is warming up and stir until the butter has melted.

Slit the vanilla bean along its length, open it out with a small, sharp
knife and scrape the tiny black seeds away from inside the pod. Add the
seeds and the pod or vanilla extract (if used) to the slow cooker pot along
with the rum and boiling water.

Add the bananas to the slow cooker pot, arranging them in a single layer
and pressing them beneath the liquid as much as you can. Cover with
the lid and cook on low for 1¹/₂–2 hours or until the bananas are hot.

Spoon the bananas and rum sauce into dishes and decorate with extra
lime rind curls and scoops of vanilla ice cream, if desired.

Drinks & preserves

Warming party mulled wines and punches are easy to make in a slow cooker. You can also make gourmet-style fruit conserves, marmalades, jellies, and savory chutneys, which make unusual and welcome gifts.

PREPARATION TIME **30 minutes**

COOKING TEMPERATURE **high**

COOKING TIME **6–7 hours**

MAKES **4 jars**

*B*eet chutney

1 bunch of raw beets, about 5 beets, trimmed and peeled

1 lb red plums, pitted and roughly chopped

1 large onion, finely chopped

1 cup red wine vinegar

1 cup light brown sugar

1½ inches fresh ginger root, peeled and finely chopped

1 tablespoon star anise pieces, crushed using a mortar and pestle

1 teaspoon peppercorns, crushed using a mortar and pestle

1 teaspoon ground cinnamon

Preheat the slow cooker if necessary; see the manufacturer's handbook. Coarsely grate the beets and put into the slow cooker pot with all the remaining ingredients.

Mix everything together thoroughly, then cover with the lid and cook on high for 6–7 hours, stirring once or twice, until the beets are tender and the plums pulpy.

Stand 4 clean jam jars in a roasting pan and warm in a low oven for 5 minutes until hot. Ladle the hot chutney into the jars, smooth the surface flat with a teaspoon, cover with waxed disks, and screw the lids in place. Label and store in a cool place until required. Once opened, store in the refrigerator. Serve with cheese, cold sliced ham or with the Zucchini & Fava Bean Frittata (see pages 48–49).

Wear rubber gloves while you're peeling the beets so that your hands don't get stained, and grate the beets in a food processor fitted with a coarse grater blade.

$\mathscr{A}$pple, thyme, &
rosemary jelly

2 lb cooking apples (not peeled or cored), washed and diced

¹/₂ cup red wine or cider vinegar

2¹/₂ cups boiling water

about 2¹/₂ cups granulated sugar

1 tablespoon thyme leaves, stripped from the stems

2 tablespoons finely chopped rosemary leaves

If you don't have a jelly bag, improvize with a large strainer set over a saucepan and line it with a new fabric dishcloth that has been rinsed with boiling water.

Preheat the slow cooker if necessary; see the manufacturer's handbook. Put the apples and vinegar into the slow cooker pot and pour over the boiling water.

Cover with the lid and cook on high for 2–3 hours until the apples are soft. Don't worry if the apples discolor slightly while cooking; this will not affect the finished jelly.

Hang a jelly bag from a frame or upturned stool and set a bowl beneath it. Ladle the cooked apple and juices into the bag and allow to drip through. Don't be tempted to press the liquid through the bag with a spoon or the finished jelly will be cloudy.

Measure the liquid and pour it into a large saucepan; for every 2¹/₂ cups liquid add 2 cups of sugar. Heat gently, stirring occasionally, until the sugar has dissolved, then boil rapidly for about 15 minutes until setting point is reached. Check with a candy thermometer or spoon a little of the jelly onto a saucer that has been chilled in the refrigerator. Leave for 1–2 minutes then run a finger through the jelly. If a finger space is left and the jelly has wrinkled it is ready; if not boil for 5–10 minutes more and then retest.

Skim any scum with a slotted spoon, then stir in the chopped herbs. Allow the jelly to stand for 5 minutes so that the herbs don't float to the surface, then ladle it into warm, dry jars. Add a waxed disk to each, cover with a cellophane jam pot cover and secure with an elastic band. Label and store in a cool place until required. Once opened, store the jelly in the refrigerator. Serve as an accompaniment to roast lamb.

PREPARATION TIME **45 minutes, plus cooling**

COOKING TEMPERATURE **low**

COOKING TIME **8–10 hours**

MAKES **6 jars of assorted sizes**

$\mathscr{O}$range marmalade

2 lb Seville oranges

5 cups boiling water

8 cups preserving or
granulated sugar

Preheat the slow cooker if necessary; see the manufacturer's handbook. Put the whole oranges into the slow cooker pot, cover with the boiling water and put an upturned saucer on top of the oranges to stop them from floating.

Cover with the lid and cook on low for 8–10 hours until the oranges are tender. Allow to cool in the slow cooker overnight.

The next day lift the oranges out of the slow cooker, draining well. Cut in quarters, scoop out and discard the seeds, then thinly slice the oranges.

Put the sliced oranges and the liquid from the slow cooker pot into a preserving pan or large saucepan, add the sugar, and heat gently, stirring occasionally until the sugar has completely dissolved.

Increase the heat, add a candy thermometer if you have one and boil for 20–30 minutes or until setting point is reached (see page 220 for how to test). Meanwhile, warm 6 jars in a warm oven.

Ladle the hot marmalade into the warm jars, cover the surface with waxed disks, add cellophane jam tops and secure with elastic bands or screw the jar lids in place. Label and store in a cool place until required.

Seville oranges are in season for only 6 weeks or so. To make a similar marmalade out of season use small oranges and add the juice of 1 lemon together with the sugar.

$\mathcal{A}$pricot conserve

1³/4 cups ready-to-eat dried apricots, diced

4 peaches, halved, pitted, and diced

1 cup superfine sugar

1¹/4 cups boiling water

Preheat the slow cooker if necessary; see the manufacturer's handbook. Put the apricots, peaches, sugar, and boiling water into the slow cooker pot and stir together.

Cover with the lid and cook on high for 3–5 hours, stirring once during cooking and then again at the end. Cook until the fruit is soft and the liquid thick and syrupy, with a texture like chutney.

Ladle the conserve into warm jars. Cover the surface with waxed disks, then a cellophane jam pot cover, and fasten with an elastic band. Allow to cool. The conserve can be stored for up to 2 months in the refrigerator.

If you would prefer to peel the peaches, cut a cross in the base of each one and plunge into boiling water for 1 minute. The skin will easily peel away.

PREPARATION TIME **15 minutes**

COOKING TEMPERATURE **low**

COOKING TIME **3–4 hours**

MAKES **3 small jars**

$\mathcal{P}$assion fruit
& lime curd

½ cup unsalted butter, diced

1¾ cups superfine sugar

4 eggs, beaten

grated zest and juice of 2 limes

grated zest of 2 lemons

juice of 1 lemon

3 passion fruit, halved

Preheat the slow cooker if necessary; see the manufacturer's handbook. Put the butter and sugar in a large bowl (double-check that it will fit into the slow cooker before you continue), then microwave for 2 minutes on full power until the butter has just melted.

Stir the sugar mix, then gradually beat in the eggs, and then the fruit zest and juice. Cover the bowl with foil and put it into the slow cooker pot. Pour boiling water into the pot to come halfway up the sides of the bowl, cover with the lid, and cook on low for 3–4 hours, stirring once during cooking, until thick.

Stir the preserve once more. Scoop the passion fruit seeds out of the halved fruit with a teaspoon and stir them into the preserve.

Ladle the preserve into warmed jars, cover the surface with waxed disks, then a cellophane jam pot cover, and fasten with an elastic band. Allow to cool. The preserve can be stored for up to 2 weeks in the refrigerator.

$\mathcal{C}$ider toddy

4 cups hard cider

¹/₂ cup whiskey

¹/₂ cup orange juice

4 tablespoons honey

2 cinnamon sticks, halved

1 orange, cut into wedges and orange rind curls, to decorate (optional)

Preheat the slow cooker if necessary; see the manufacturer's handbook. Add all the ingredients to the slow cooker pot, cover with the lid, and cook on high for 1 hour.

Reduce the heat and cook on low for 2–3 hours until piping hot. Stir, then ladle into heatproof tumblers. Add orange wedges and curls to decorate, if desired.

PREPARATION TIME **5 minutes**

COOKING TEMPERATURE **high
and low**

COOKING TIME **3–4 hours**

SERVES **6**

ℳulled wine

**3 cups or 1 bottle inexpensive
red wine**

1¼ cups clear apple juice

1¼ cups water

juice of 1 orange

1 orange, sliced

½ lemon, sliced

1 cinnamon stick, halved

6 cloves

2 bay leaves

Preheat the slow cooker if necessary; see the manufacturer's handbook. Pour the wine, apple juice, water, and orange juice into the slow cooker pot. Add the sliced orange and lemon, the cinnamon stick, cloves, and bay leaves, then mix in the sugar and brandy.

Cover with the lid and cook on high for 1 hour. Reduce to low and cook for 3–4 hours.

$\mathscr{H}$ot spiced berry punch

4 cups cranberry and raspberry drink

2 cups frozen berry fruits

¹/₄ cup superfine sugar

4 tablespoons crème de cassis
(optional)

4 small star anise

1 cinnamon stick, halved lengthwise

fresh raspberries, to decorate
(optional)

Preheat the slow cooker if necessary; see the manufacturer's handbook. Pour the cranberry and raspberry drink into the slow cooker pot, add the frozen fruits, the sugar, and crème de cassis (if used). Stir together, then add the star anise and halved cinnamon stick. Cover with the lid and cook on high for 1 hour.

Reduce the heat to low and cook for 2–3 hours. Strain if desired, then take out the star anise and cinnamon and add these to serving tumblers. Pour the hot punch into small heatproof glasses and add a few fresh raspberries, if desired.

This is an adaptable drink for parties. For a nonalcoholic, driver-friendly version, omit the cassis. You can also omit the cassis and puree the drink until smooth for a warming toddy for children or you could make a cider-, fruit juice, or tea-based punch instead.

PREPARATION TIME **5 minutes**

COOKING TEMPERATURE **high and low**

COOKING TIME **3–4 hours**

SERVES **6**

$\mathcal{H}$ot buttered rum

4 cups clear apple juice

²/₃ cup dark rum

2 tablespoons honey

2 tablespoons dark brown sugar

2 tablespoons butter

6 cloves

1 dessert apple, cored and
    thickly sliced, to decorate

Preheat the slow cooker if necessary; see the manufacturer's handbook. Pour the apple juice, rum, honey, sugar, butter, and cloves into the slow cooker pot.

Cover with the lid and cook on high for 1 hour. Reduce the heat and cook on low for 3–4 hours. Stir, scoop out the cloves then ladle the punch into heatproof tumblers. Decorate with slices of apple.

PREPARATION TIME **10 minutes**

COOKING TEMPERATURE **low**

COOKING TIME **2–3 hours**

SERVES **4**

Skier's hot chocolate

4 oz good quality chocolate

2 tablespoons superfine sugar

3 cups whole milk

few drops of vanilla extract

little ground cinnamon

3 tablespoons kahlua coffee liqueur (optional)

mini marshmallows, to serve

Preheat the slow cooker if necessary; see the manufacturer's handbook. Place the chocolate and sugar in the slow cooker pot, then add the milk, vanilla extract, and cinnamon.

Cover with the lid and cook on low for 2–3 hours, stirring once or twice, until the chocolate has melted and the drink is hot. Stir in the kahlua, if using. Ladle into cups and top with a few mini marshmallows.

Ways to cheat

In an ideal world we would all like to make supper from scratch every day, but most of us just don't have the time. The recipes in this chapter include some easy shortcuts using pantry ingredients combined with a few ready-made sauces and chilled convenience foods.

PREPARATION TIME **15 minutes**

COOKING TEMPERATURE **low**

COOKING TIME **6–7 hours**

SERVES **4**

$\mathscr{M}$eatballs & tagliatelle

1 tablespoon olive oil

2 x 11½ oz packages of 12 beef
meatballs

1 onion, chopped

13 oz jar roasted vegetable and
tomato pasta sauce

¾ cup red wine

12 oz tagliatelle

small bunch of basil (optional)

chunk of Parmesan cheese, grated
or shaved, to serve

Preheat the slow cooker if necessary; see the manufacturer's handbook. Heat the oil in a large skillet, add the meatballs and fry, in batches if necessary, until browned but not cooked through. Scoop out of the pan with a slotted spoon and transfer to the slow cooker pot.

Add the onion to the skillet and fry, stirring, for 5 minutes or until softened. Drain off most of the fat, then pour in the pasta sauce and red wine. Bring the mixture to a boil, stirring, then pour over the meatballs.

Cover with the lid and cook on low for 6–7 hours. Just before serving put the pasta in a large saucepan of boiling water and cook for 9–10 minutes until just tender. Drain in a colander.

Tear the basil leaves, if using, over the meatballs in the slow cooker, add the drained pasta and toss together. Spoon into shallow bowls and serve sprinkled with some grated or shaved Parmesan.

Ready-made meatballs are an excellent secret ingredient. Mix any jar of pasta sauce, some red wine, and basil and you can create an easy supper that is smart enough to serve to friends. If you are making this for children use beef stock instead of the wine.

PREPARATION TIME **15 minutes**

COOKING TEMPERATURE **low**

COOKING TIME **7–8 hours**

SERVES **4**

Chicken with thyme
& mushroom sauce

2 tablespoons butter

1 tablespoon olive oil

4 boneless, skinless chicken breasts, about 1¼ lb in total

1 small onion, thinly sliced

3 cups sliced button mushrooms

13½ oz can cream of chicken soup

2 tablespoons sherry

1–2 sprigs of thyme

TO SERVE

new potatoes

broccoli

Preheat the slow cooker if necessary; see the manufacturer's handbook. Heat half the butter and the oil in a skillet, add the chicken breasts and fry briefly until browned on both sides. Lift out of the pan with a slotted spoon and transfer to the slow cooker pot.

Add the onion to the pan and fry, stirring, for 5 minutes or until softened. Add the remaining butter and the mushrooms and fry for 2–3 minutes.

Pour in the soup and sherry and bring to a boil. Add the thyme to the slow cooker pot and pour the soup mixture over the top.

Cover with the lid and cook on low for 7–8 hours or until the chicken is tender. Test by inserting a small knife into the center of one of the breasts in the center of the pot; if the juices run clear they are ready. Spoon onto plates, discard the thyme, and serve with new potatoes and steamed broccoli.

A can of soup can be used as a substitute for a homemade sauce. Chicken soup has been used in this recipe, but you could use tomato, mixed vegetable, or mushroom.

$\mathcal{L}$amb stew
with dumplings

1 tablespoon sunflower oil

1¼ lb lamb leg steaks

1 leek, sliced; white and green parts
kept separate

2 carrots, diced

2 x 13½ oz cans Scotch broth

6¼ oz package herby dumpling mix

5–6 tablespoons water

Preheat the slow cooker if necessary; see the manufacturer's handbook. Heat the oil in a skillet, add the lamb, and fry until browned on both sides. Lift out with a slotted spoon and transfer to the slow cooker pot.

Add the white leek slices to the skillet and cook for 2–3 minutes until just softened. Add the carrots and cans of soup, bring to a boil, stirring, then pour over the lamb. Cover with the lid and cook on low for 8–10 hours.

When almost ready to serve, tip the dumpling mix into a bowl. Using a fork, gradually mix in enough water to make a soft but not sticky dough. Divide into 8 and roll each piece into a ball.

Stir the green leek slices into the casserole, arrange the dumplings on top, replace the lid, and cook on high for 30 minutes until the dumplings are well risen and the tops are dry. Spoon the stew and dumplings into shallow bowls to serve.

Lamb leg steaks have been used in this recipe for speed, but if you prefer you could buy shoulder steaks or boned rib of lamb and slice or dice it before frying.

PREPARATION TIME **15 minutes**

COOKING TEMPERATURE **low**

COOKING TIME 8–9 **hours**

SERVES **4**

Chinese spiced beef

2 tablespoons sunflower oil

1½ lb ready-diced stewing beef

1 onion, thinly sliced

1 inch fresh ginger root, peeled and finely chopped

14 oz jar hoisin and five spice cook-in sauce

8½ oz package ready-prepared stir-fry vegetable mix

2 scallions, thinly sliced

12½ oz package chilled egg noodles

small bunch of cilantro

Preheat the slow cooker if necessary; see the manufacturer's handbook. Heat 1 tablespoon oil in a skillet, add the beef, a few pieces at a time, until all the pieces are in the pan, then fry, stirring, until browned all over. Scoop the meat out of the pan with a slotted spoon and transfer it to the slow cooker pot.

Add the onion to the pan and fry, stirring, for 5 minutes or until it is just beginning to brown. Stir in the ginger, then add the jar of cook-in sauce. Bring to a boil, stirring, then pour into the slow cooker pot. Cover with the lid and cook on low for 8–9 hours until the beef is tender.

When almost ready to serve, heat the remaining oil in a clean skillet, add the stir-fry mix and scallions, and cook for 3–4 minutes until just beginning to soften. Push the vegetables to one side of the pan. Add the noodles and cook for 2–3 minutes until hot.

Spoon the noodles into shallow bowls, stir the beef, and spoon on top. Serve sprinkled with the vegetables and torn cilantro leaves.

Use this recipe as a basis and adapt it as you wish, adding other flavored ready-made sauces. There should be enough liquid to just cover the meat, but if there is not add a little extra boiling water or a splash of wine or cider.

Cauliflower &
spinach balti

1 tablespoon sunflower oil

1 onion, chopped

1 lb 3 oz can balti curry sauce

1 large cauliflower, core discarded and florets cut into large pieces (about 1½ lb prepared weight)

13½ oz can green lentils, drained

3 cups spinach, washed and torn into pieces

naan bread, to serve

Preheat the slow cooker if necessary; see the manufacturer's handbook. Heat the oil in a skillet, add the onion and fry, stirring, for 5 minutes or until softened. Add the curry sauce and bring to a boil.

Add the cauliflower and lentils to the slow cooker pot. Pour over the hot sauce, cover with the lid, and cook on low for 5–6 hours or until the cauliflower is tender.

Stir the cauliflower and sprinkle the spinach on top. Replace the lid and cook, still on low, for 10–15 minutes until the spinach is just wilted. Spoon into bowls and serve with warm naan bread.

The amount of liquid and size of vegetable chunk greatly affects the speed of cooking in a slow cooker. The more liquid there is and the smaller the size of the vegetable chunks, the quicker the cooking.

Mediterranean
shepherd's pie

2 tablespoons olive oil

1 onion, chopped

1 eggplant, diced

1 lb ground lamb

2 garlic cloves, finely chopped

13 oz jar tomato pasta sauce

1 zucchini, diced

1 lb 10 oz package chilled
    ready-made mashed potato

4 tablespoons freshly grated
    Parmesan or cheddar cheese

Preheat the slow cooker if necessary; see the manufacturer's handbook. Heat the oil in a skillet, add the onion and eggplant and fry for 5 minutes, stirring until softened. Scoop the mixture out of the pan with a slotted spoon and transfer to the slow cooker pot.

Add the lamb to the skillet and dry-fry, stirring, for 5 minutes until browned. Add the garlic and pasta sauce and bring to a boil, stirring.

Add the zucchini to the slow cooker pot and pour the sauce over the top. Cover and cook on low for 8–10 hours.

When almost ready to serve, microwave the mashed potato, following the instructions on the package. Stir the mash and stir the meat with separate spoons, then spoon the potato over the top of the meat. Sprinkle with grated cheese, then lift the slow cooker pot out of the machine housing with oven mitts. Brown the pie under a preheated hot broiler and serve with peas.

PREPARATION TIME **15 minutes**

COOKING TEMPERATURE **low**

COOKING TIME **4–4½ hours**

SERVES **4**

Chocolate croissant
& pecan pudding

¼ cup butter

4 chocolate croissants

¼ cup superfine sugar

¼ teaspoon ground cinnamon

⅓ cup pecan nuts, roughly crushed

1¼ cups whole milk

2 whole eggs

2 egg yolks

1 teaspoon vanilla extract

cream, to serve

Grease the inside of a 5 cup straight-sided ovenproof dish with a little of the butter (checking first that the dish will fit into your slow cooker).

Thickly slice the croissants and spread one side of each slice with the remaining butter. Mix together the sugar and spice. Arrange the croissants in layers in the dish, sprinkling each layer with the spiced sugar and the pecans.

Beat the milk, eggs, and egg yolks with the vanilla extract. Pour into the dish and allow to soak for 15 minutes. Preheat the slow cooker if necessary; see the manufacturer's handbook.

Loosely cover the top of the pudding with buttered foil, then lower it into the slow cooker pot. Pour boiling water into the pot to come halfway up the sides of the dish, cover with the lid, and cook on low for 4–4½ hours or until the custard is set and the pudding well risen.

Lift the dish out of the slow cooker with oven mitts. Scoop into bowls and serve with cream.

For a more traditional bread and butter pudding, use 4 slices of buttered bread and sprinkle the layers with sugar and a few spoonfuls of dried fruit instead of the cinnamon and pecans. Make up the custard with vanilla extract.

PREPARATION TIME **15 minutes**

COOKING TEMPERATURE **high**

COOKING TIME **3–3½ hours**

SERVES **4–6**

Cherry & coconut
sponge pudding

butter, for greasing

½ cup shredded coconut

13 oz can cherry pie filling

1 lb package pound cake mix

4 tablespoons sunflower oil or 1 egg
(see cake mix instructions)

vanilla ice cream, to serve (optional)

Preheat the slow cooker if necessary; see the manufacturer's handbook. Lightly butter a 6 cup pudding mold and line the base with a circle of waxed or nonstick parchment paper. Sprinkle in a little of the coconut, then tilt and turn the basin until the buttery sides are lightly coated. Spoon half the cherry pie filling into the bottom of the mold.

Tip the cake mix into a bowl and mix in the oil or egg and water as the instructions on the package direct.

Stir in the remaining coconut, then spoon into the mold and level the surface. Cover the top with a piece of buttered foil, making a fold in the center, or doming up the top slightly, to allow the pudding to rise. Tie the foil in place with string and lower the basin into the slow cooker pot.

Pour boiling water into the slow cooker pot to come halfway up the sides of the basin, cover with the lid, and cook on high for 3–3½ hours or until the pudding is well risen, feels dry, and springs back when pressed with a fingertip.

Remove the mold from the slow cooker pot with oven mitts and loosen the edge of the pudding with a round-bladed knife. Turn out onto a plate, remove the mold, and peel away the lining paper. Warm the remaining pie filling in a microproof bowl in a microwave for 45–60 seconds on full power until hot. Serve the pudding with the remaining cherries and scoops of vanilla ice cream, if desired.

Mix and match your own flavor combinations by using a chocolate cake mix or a can of apple pie filling livened up with some grated lemon or orange zest.

PREPARATION TIME **15 minutes**

COOKING TEMPERATURE **low**

COOKING TIME **2–3 hours**

SERVES **4**

$\mathcal{R}$aspberry & rhubarb
oaty crumble

13 oz trimmed rhubarb

1¼ cups frozen raspberries

¼ cup superfine sugar

3 tablespoons water

thick cream, to serve

TOPPING

1 tablespoon butter

3 tablespoons slivered almonds

7 oz, about 4, ready-made fruit and nut bars

Preheat the slow cooker if necessary; see the manufacturer's handbook. Cut the rhubarb into 1 inch thick slices and add to the slow cooker pot with the still-frozen raspberries, the sugar, and water.

Cover with the lid and cook on low for 2–3 hours until the rhubarb is just tender.

When almost ready to serve, heat the butter in a skillet, add the almonds and crumble in the fruit and nut bars. Fry, stirring, for 3–4 minutes until hot and lightly browned.

Spoon the fruit into bowls, sprinkle the crumble over the top, and serve with thick cream.

*T*offee apple pancakes

¼ cup butter

⅓ cup light brown sugar

2 tablespoons light corn syrup

4 dessert apples, cored and each cut into 8 slices

juice of 1 lemon

12 oz package or 6 chilled or long-life pancakes

grated chocolate, to decorate (optional)

vanilla ice cream, to serve

Preheat the slow cooker if necessary; see the manufacturer's handbook. Heat the butter, sugar, and syrup in a microproof bowl in a microwave for 1–1½ minutes on full power until the butter has just melted.

Add the apples and lemon juice to the slow cooker pot and toss together. Stir the butter mix and pour it over the apple. Cover with the lid and cook on high for 1–1½ hours.

Heat the pancakes in a microwave according to the instructions on the back of the package. Fold in half and arrange on serving plates. Stir the apple mix, then spoon it onto the pancakes. Top with a scoop of vanilla ice cream and sprinkle with a little grated chocolate, if desired.

For those of you who really like chocolate, coat the pancakes with a little chocolate spread before microwaving, and then top with the apples and toffee sauce.

251

Index

Acknowledgments

Executive Editor Eleanor Maxfield

Senior Editor Charlotte Macey

Executive Art Editor Penny Stock

Designer Barbara Zuñiga

Senior Production Controller Amanda Mackie

Photographer Stephen Conroy

Food Stylist Sara Lewis

Props Stylist Liz Hippisley

Special Photography: © Octopus Publishing Group Limited/Stephen Conroy